DATE DUE

JACK KEROUAC

Recent Titles in Greenwood Biographies

JACK KEROUAC

A Biography

Michael J. Dittman

GREENWOOD BIOGRAPHIES

GREENWOOD PRESS
WESTPORT, CONNECTICUT · LONDON

Library of Congress Cataloging-in-Publication Data

Dittman, Michael J.
  Jack Kerouac : a biography / Michael J. Dittman.
    p. cm. — (Greenwood biographies, ISSN 1540–4900)
    Includes bibliographical references (p.   ).
    ISBN 0–313–32836–6 (alk. paper)
    1. Kerouac, Jack, 1922–1969. 2. Authors, American—
20th century—Biography. 3. Beat generation—Biography.
I. Title. II. Series.
PS3521.E735Z628   2004
813'.54—dc22   2004009233
British Library Cataloguing in Publication Data is available.

Library of Congress Catalog Card Number: 2004009233
ISBN: 0–313–32836–6
ISSN: 1540–4900

First published in 2004

Greenwood Press, 88 Post Road West, Westport, CT 06881
An imprint of Greenwood Publishing Group, Inc.
www.greenwood.com

Printed in the United States of America

♾️™

The paper used in this book complies with the
Permanent Paper Standard issued by the National
Information Standards Organization (Z39.48–1984).

10 9 8 7 6 5 4 3 2 1

CONTENTS

CONTENTS

Photo essay follows page 62

SERIES FOREWORD

In response to high school and public library needs, Greenwood developed this distinguished series of full-length biographies specifically for student use. Prepared by field experts and professionals, these engaging biographies are tailored for high school students who need challenging yet accessible biographies. Ideal for secondary school assignments, the length, format and subject areas are designed to meet educators' requirements and students' interests.

Greenwood offers an extensive selection of biographies spanning all curriculum related subject areas including social studies, the sciences, literature and the arts, history and politics, as well as popular culture, covering public figures and famous personalities from all time periods and backgrounds, both historic and contemporary, who have made an impact on American and/or world culture. Greenwood biographies were chosen based on comprehensive feedback from librarians and educators. Consideration was given to both curriculum relevance and inherent interest. The result is an intriguing mix of the well known and the unexpected, the saints and sinners from long-ago history and contemporary pop culture. Readers will find a wide array of subject choices from fascinating crime figures like Al Capone to inspiring pioneers like Margaret Mead, from the greatest minds of our time like Stephen Hawking to the most amazing success stories of our day like J. K. Rowling.

While the emphasis is on fact, not glorification, the books are meant to be fun to read. Each volume provides in-depth information about the subject's life from birth through childhood, the teen years, and adulthood. A thorough account relates family background and education, traces personal and professional influences, and explores struggles, accomplishments, and contributions. A timeline highlights the most significant life events against a historical perspective. Bibliographies supplement the reference value of each volume.

INTRODUCTION

When Jack Kerouac, being examined by a navy psychiatrist, was asked to explain what the doctor had termed Kerouac's bizarre behavior, he responded happily that he was committed to "dedicating my actions to experience in order to write about them, sacrificing myself on the altar of Art." Sacrifice himself he did, from the year he was born to French Canadian immigrants in the city of Lowell, Massachusetts, on March 12, 1922, until he died, bitter, angry, and alcoholic, on October 21, 1969, in Saint Petersburg, Florida.

As a youth, Kerouac was not only highly intelligent but also physically gifted, earning a football scholarship to Columbia University. After his freshman year, Kerouac dropped out of Columbia, signing up for a hitch with the U.S. Merchant Marine, then attempting to join the navy. After finding that navy discipline was too much for him, he claimed insanity and took therapy sessions with the aforementioned psychiatrist, earning an honorable discharge for "indifferent character." He then headed back to New York City, where he met the people who star in On the Road: Allen Ginsberg as Carlo Marx, William S. Burroughs as Old Bull Lee, and, perhaps most important, a 20-year-old ex-con named Neal Cassady, who would appear in the book as Dean Moriarty.

Inspired by this group, Kerouac offered his sacrifice on the altar of art in the form of forsaking middle-class America for a life of varied experience, turning his life into roman à clef fictions. In all his books, but most famously in On the Road, Kerouac preferred not to characterize his work as fiction, or striving to create invented experiences. Instead he said that he was creating his text by letting his imagination embellish remembered events. *On the Road* was first deemed unpublishable, not only because of its reliance on a writing style Kerouac called "spontaneous prose" and the reluctance of some of the individuals who appeared in the book to sign libel waivers, but also because of the narrator Sal's empathy and longing for the life of the downtrodden and disenfranchised. Kerouac felt that the ancestor of the white hipster of the 1950s was the African American jazzman, or African American culture more generally, and, to some extent, that of other minority races.

Six years passed before the book was published, and its publication marked the beginning of the end of a normal life for Kerouac. In the late 1940s, the term "Beat" acquired a glamour, and pseudobeatniks were slated to appear in movies and on TV, all claiming Kerouac as their spiritual father. These caricatures, though, misrepresented what Kerouac felt was meant by the term "Beat," a word that he always linked to the word "beatific," or sanctified. Always a shy man, he found that he could not explain himself to reporters. He clashed with fans who showed up at his house to party all night, looking for Salvatore Paradise and Dean Moriarty. As an escape, Kerouac turned increasingly to bottles of Johnny Walker Red, confessing to his friend and fellow Beat writer John Clellon Holmes, "I can't stand to meet anybody anymore. They talk to me like I wasn't me."[1]

Kerouac's nomadic lifestyle continued all his life as he sought peace and satisfaction. He and his mother moved repeatedly. He married three times, fathering a number of children. With each move, his alcoholism worsened, and although his desperate efforts to dry out in California are recorded in his novel *Big Sur*, he could not break free from his addiction. He died, from a stomach hemorrhage, in the Florida home that he and his mother shared. It was a night in October, in the fall, a time that Sal Paradise, Kerouac's alter ego in *On the Road*, said always made him feel like moving somewhere new.

NOTE

1. "Jack Kerouac." *Contemporary Authors*. Vol. 54 (Chicago: Gale/Thompson, 2004), p. 241.

TIMELINE OF EVENTS IN
THE LIFE OF JACK KEROUAC

1922   Jack Kerouac is born in Lowell, Massachusetts, on March 12.

1939   He graduates from Lowell High School.

1941   In New York, he attends Columbia College on a football scholarship.

1944   Kerouac meets Lucien Carr, Allen Ginsberg, and William S. Burroughs.

1945   He begins writing *The Town and the City* and meets Neal Cassady for the first time in New York.

1946   Kerouac collaborates with William Burroughs on *And the Hippos Were Boiled in Their Tanks*.

1947   He travels to Denver, California, and back to New York.

1949   He travels with Cassady to Louisiana and San Francisco and briefly lives in Colorado. He returns with Cassady to New York.

1950   Kerouac's road trips inspire him to begin working on the earliest version of *On the Road*. *The Town and the City* is published, and Kerouac once again travels to Denver. In Denver, he meets up with Cassady, and together they take a trip to Mexico.

1951   Kerouac begins the third version of *On the Road*, typing the draft on a single roll of paper in three weeks. He discovers "spontaneous prose" and begins to rewrite *On the Road*. He lives at Neal Cassady's home in San Francisco.

1952   Kerouac writes *Dr. Sax* in Mexico City while staying in William Burroughs's apartment. He travels to North Carolina to visit his sister, then heads back to California. While he is in California and

Mexico, he begins to write *The Railroad Earth*. He returns to New York.

1953   Kerouac travels to California and ends up in New Orleans after leaving the ship he had been employed to work on. When he arrives back in New York, he writes *The Subterraneans*.

1954   He returns to San Jose to visit the Cassadys, then back to New York. Once again, he travels to California, and while in San Francisco, he writes *San Francisco Blues*. *Some of the Dharma* is written during his stays in New York and North Carolina.

1955   Kerouac travels to Mexico City, where he writes *Mexico City Blues* and begins *Tristessa*. He attends Ginsberg's first public reading of *Howl* in San Francisco.

1956   While in North Carolina, he writes *Visions of Gerard*. Kerouac again heads to California and then to Washington, where he writes *The Scripture of the Golden Eternity* and *Old Angel Midnight*. He begins writing in a journal that would later become book 1 of *Desolation Angels*. *Tristessa* is finished in Mexico City. He returns to New York.

1957   Kerouac travels to Tangier, Morocco, Paris, and London. He returns to New York, then moves to Berkeley. He visits Mexico City, then moves to Orlando, Florida. He returns to New York, and at this time, *On the Road* is published. In Orlando, he writes *The Dharma Bums*.

1958   Kerouac buys a home in Long Island; *The Subterraneans* and *The Dharma Bums* are published. He begins writing sketches for *Lonesome Traveler*.

1959   *Dr. Sax*, *Mexico City Blues*, and *Maggie Cassidy* are published. Kerouac travels to Los Angeles and appears on *The Steve Allen Show*.

1960   He travels to California and, while there, suffers alcohol withdrawal and a nervous breakdown. He returns to New York, and *Tristessa* and *Lonesome Traveler* are published.

1961   Kerouac's *Book of Dreams* is published. He moves to Orlando, Florida, and while in Mexico City, he writes book 2 ("Passing Through") of *Desolation Angels*. After his return to Florida, he writes *Big Sur*.

1962   *Big Sur* is published.

1963   *Visions of Gerard* is published.

1964   Kerouac moves back to Florida. In New York, he sees Neal Cassady, whom he has not seen in years.

1965   Kerouac travels to Paris, France, where he writes *Satori in Paris*. When he returns to Florida, he writes *Pic*. *Desolation Angels* is published.

1966   *Satori in Paris* is published. Kerouac moves to Hyannis, Massachusetts.

1967   He moves to Lowell, Massachusetts, and writes *Vanity of Duluoz*.

1968   Neal Cassady dies in Mexico. *Vanity of Duluoz* is published. Kerouac travels to Europe, and when he returns to the United States, he moves to Saint Petersburg, Florida.

1969   At the age of 47, Jack Kerouac dies in Saint Petersburg on October 21 of an abdominal hemorrhage.

Chapter 1

YOUTH

Today Lowell, Massachusetts, is part of the ever-expanding rust belt of cities that fill the northeastern United States. The mills that churned out textiles and other goods are long closed, leaving the city quiet. Along with the specter of dead industry, the ghost and influence of Kerouac spread themselves across the city. The Merrimack River, a touchstone for the young Jack Kerouac, runs through downtown Lowell, Main Street following along it. The Lowell High School, built of yellow stone with a large clock, would be immortalized in Kerouac's *Maggie Cassidy*, as well in Lowell lore when the adult Kerouac showed up there, crippled by drink to give a "lecture" to one of the school's literature classes. The Pollard Memorial Library, surrounded by gray, flat-looking official buildings, is distinguished by the cannon outside and by the fact that young Kerouac would skip classes to come here and read, to create his own education. The local newspaper, where Kerouac worked as a sportswriter for several months, is still the *Lowell Sun*. For a man who became famous for recording his adventurous travels, Kerouac always closely associated himself with his hometown, and because of that, the town bears his imprint.

Toward the end of his life, Kerouac would grow obsessive about his family tree, to the extent that he was pulled in by a slick-talking, greasy-haired Lowell con man who claimed to have proof that Kerouac was the rightful chief of a Canadian Native American tribe. Mostly, though, he thought about the family roots he believed were to be found in France.

Jack inherited this obsession from his father, Leo, who told him that he had aristocratic blood, that before the time of Christ, the Kerouac ancestors had traveled to Cornwall, England, from Celtic Ireland, and that

"Kerouac" was actually a Gaelic word, *kerousc'h*, meaning "language of the house," and that the family crest was gold stripes on a blue field with three silver nails and the motto "Love, work, and suffer." Kerouac would spend much of his life and produce many of his books in an effort to capture his fascination with the family saga that was introduced to him so early in life. In his book *Lonesome Traveler*, he writes that his family originally hailed from the Breton region in France. He continues to say that in 1750, Baron Alexandre Louis Lebris de Kerouac of Cornwall, England, was given land in Canada, among the Mohawk and Caughnawaga tribes, where the Kerouacs became potato farmers.

Jack's grandfather was the first Kerouac to come to the United States. Jean-Baptiste, a carpenter, moved to Nashua, New Hampshire, in the mid-1800s. The French Canadian culture in America was one separate from the country in which it resided. Already-established New Englanders despised the French Canadians who made their way into the mill towns and logging camps at the turn of the nineteenth century. They were renowned for being strong, willing workers who would undertake a 72-hour workweek in the mills without a word of protest. At the same time, the French Canadians organized themselves into ghettos, where they kept their ways and language and didn't mix with their neighbors. Critics have suggested that this tradition of valuing the interior world over the exterior helped to create the rich fantasy life that the young Jack Kerouac would draw on and eventually use to make his way in the world.

Jean-Baptiste sent his son, Leo, off to private school in Rhode Island, where he soon grew to be a good-looking young man—and, by all accounts, a ladies' man. He also had skills as a writer and printer. Using both talents in one of his first jobs, he helped to bring back to life a defunct French-language newspaper, *L'Etoile*, in the thriving mill town of Lowell, where he had decided to settle.

At age 26, Leo met Gabrielle Levesque, an orphan who worked in a shoe shop. They married, set up housekeeping in Lowell, and began a family. Times were difficult. Leo had a short temper and an overinflated sense of self-worth. When he felt snubbed at *L'Etoile*, he left the paper and struck out on his own, starting a small press, Spotlight Print, to create bills and programs for the local theaters and burlesque houses. At the same time, he also started a small entertainment paper, called the *Spotlight*, which featured reviews and news of local theater comings and goings, all written by Leo himself.

When Jean Louis Kerouac was born on March 12, 1922, Lowell was a very different place than it is today. Even though only a decade later the Great Depression would force more than 40 percent of Lowell's employable citizens to seek some sort of government aid, in 1922 the town hummed with activity. By the time Jack was born, Leo had become a successful businessman. His paper, the *Spotlight*, and its theater articles brought free tickets, and young Jack was privy to the world of the cinema Western and the boozy vaudevillian subculture. It's easy to see how this sort of environment played a part in Kerouac's later development, with its emphasis on hard work, artistic expression, and the longing for home in a small town. The Kerouacs had a strong dedication to family, but at the same time, a desperation that so many small-town adolescents feel—that they are undervalued by the town's citizens and that to come to love the place they are from, they must first break away from it.

Kerouac was the last of three children; his sister Carolyn (known by her family nickname of Nin) was the middle child, and Gerard, his sickly brother, was the oldest. As an adult, Kerouac would claim that he could remember the day of his birth. "I remember that afternoon. . . . I perceived it through beads hanging in a door and through lace curtains and glass of a universal sad lost redness of mortal damnation."[1] He was born at home, in a room on the top floor of the house on Lupine Road in Lowell where the Kerouacs were living at the time. When Jack was born, Carolyn was three years old, and Gerard was five. Gerard was diagnosed with rheumatic fever, and slowly but surely, as the family watched helplessly, he died from the disease.

Gerard's death had a dramatic, long-lasting effect on Jack. Although his older brother was sickly and weak, Jack idolized him, seeing in his quiet gentleness a reflection of the Catholic saints that he learned about through the work of the Saint Louis parish, which lay just one block away from his home at 34 Beaulieu Street. The Roman Catholic Church held a firm grip on the lives of its working-class French Canadian parishioners, reinforcing separatism by the encouragement of old traditions and the use of the old language referred to in the dialect as *joule*. For Gerard especially, sickly, devout, obsessed by Saint Therese de Lisieux, who taught the seeking of good through a childlike innocence and who also died young from consumption, the church provided much of his contact with the outside world.

With the importance of the church looming large in young Jack's life and his brother's high place in the local church as an emblem of a holy innocent, Gerard in turn took up a mythical place in Kerouac's life. In Gerard's intercession to save a mouse's life after it was caught in a trap, and in his coaxing sparrows to his bedside window, Jack saw saintliness, reinforced by the near-constant visits to Gerard's bedside of nuns and parish priests. Kerouac eventually claimed that the sparrows knew Gerard by name, à la Saint Francis of Assisi, and that they would flock to his windowsill when he was especially sick. Adding to the magic was the story of Gerard expounding on a vision of heaven he saw when asked a simple question in his catechism class. Relating the incident in his book about his bother, *Visions of Gerard*, Kerouac writes:

> "My sister, I saw the Virgin Mary."
> The nun is stunned...
> "She told me to come on—and there was a pretty little white wagon with two little lambs to pull it and we started out and we were going to heaven...and two white pigeons on my shoulder—doves and she asked me 'Where were you Gerard, we've been waiting for you all morning...don't be afraid my good sister, we're all in Heaven—but we don't know it!'—
> "Oh," he laughs, "*we don't know it!*"[2]

Although Gerard was confined to his sickbed at this point, Jack saw him as a hero who kept his younger brother entertained with stories and drawings. At the same time, Kerouac's adulation of his older brother set up an impossible standard. Priests and nuns flocked to Gerard's bedside to comfort him, even more frequently when he couldn't go to school anymore. Jack and his mother spread holy cards around Gerard, and although there was no positive effect on Gerard, all these things made a strong mental impression on Jack. To him, the more the clergy visited and the more the family enshrined Gerard, the more Jack became convinced that there was something different about his brother, something holy; he became convinced that his brother was a saint, taking on the sins of the world, and taking on Jack's sins as well. Kerouac began to believe that Gerard was dying so that the family could have a fuller life.

Gerard's death on July 8, 1926, snapped the Kerouac family like a twig. Leo, to the horror of Gabrielle, lost his faith and quit going to Mass and following the rules and rituals of the Catholic faith. Gabrielle broke mentally and began verbally attacking Jack for not being more like Gerard, even suggesting that young Jack had somehow been responsible for Gerard's death. Gerard had always been kind, quiet, and slow to anger, but Jack was a normal young boy—rambunctious, loud, careless at times. It must have been a difficult, psychologically exhausting, and eventually futile task to compete with a ghost. Thirty years later, Kerouac would write, "there's no doubt in my mind that my mother loves Gerard more than she loves me."[3]

By 1930, the Kerouacs, who always seemed to be in the process of pack-ing or unpacking, moved into a house (which showed up decades later in Kerouac's *Book of Dreams*) at 66 West Street in Lowell. Jack loved this house for the solidity of the huge furniture and hearth, and, most impor-tant, a statue of Saint Therese that Gabrielle made sure was already there when they moved in. Jack began to believe that the statue turned its head as he walked past, as he had seen in a movie in school. Gabrielle did noth-ing to discourage the vision and, in fact, attempted to connect it with Gerard.

This homemade sanctification of Gerard draws on a long French Cana-dian tradition of child saints including Marie-Rose Ferron, a Quebecois girl who was reputed to have the stigmata. Ferron was a favorite in the Ker-ouac household, as was her admonishment, "Death is only a passage that leads to life."[4] Indeed, Kerouac scholar Gerald Nicosia believes that this statement, which he claims was common in the Kerouac household as Jack was growing up, not only helped to set some of Kerouac's ideas about death (and ironically helped lay the groundwork for some of the quasi-Catholic beliefs that would lead him to study Buddhism, eventually claiming that Buddha and Christ are equal) but also served to confuse the death of the gentle Gerard with the hagiographic life of Marie-Rose Ferron.

While Jack and his mother turned more and more inward with each move, Leo continued to seek his fortune in the expanded community, be-yond the French Canadian ghetto. In the fall of 1930, he opened a boxing gym. Soon, however, he was losing money hand over fist because of the small crowds his fight cards would draw. Never one to miss an opportunity, he instead turned his boxers into professional wrestlers, an entertainment that was enjoying one of its periodic bouts of popularity, and even hired one of his athletes to be his personal driver. Like many of Leo's entrepre-neurial plans, however, the gym soon went bankrupt, and Leo was back on the streets looking for printing work. For Jack, though, the image of these larger-than-life men stayed in his head, in the depths of his psyche, to bubble up in what he saw as one of his major works, *Dr. Sax*.

In the fall of 1932, Jack met one of the great friends and confidants of his life, a Jesuit priest named Armand "Spike" Morrisette. Morrisette him-self was a character, a supporter of Kerouac and Lowell in general, so much so, in fact, that a Lowell street was named after him following his death. Rumors spun around Father Spike, and the thespian in him loved it. People said that he had been a chaplain in the French navy and a priest to the Rockettes, that he had baby-sat the Nixon children, and that as a 12-year-old he had given flowers to an appreciative, albeit Protestant, Bette Davis.

At the same time that Jack met Father Morrisette, he was also so recognized for his academic ability that he skipped the sixth grade, moving directly from fifth to seventh, and also became an altar boy at Saint Jean Baptiste Cathedral. Morrisette would recall later in interviews that Jack seemed too nervous and worried for a boy his age, and that he also began to believe that Jack would make a fine Jesuit priest. Kerouac even believed that he had seen a vision, perhaps of Gerard.

Alongside Father Morrisette was another Kerouac supporter, his new teacher Helen Mansfield, whom he met in the fall of 1933. For the first time, Kerouac was attending a school where he was required to submit all his work and carry on all his discussions in English. Because his prior education had been in French, Kerouac kept quiet in class. Out of school, however, he had begun to blossom, especially with his French Canadian friends. He began to take on a role that he would never repeat in the rest of his life—the leader, the man at the head of a small group, the idea man who convinces others to carry out his plans. He was always landing on his feet, depending on his growing athleticism and bravery to cover up the difficulty he had keeping up with all the English-language work that was so unfamiliar to him. Even with all his trouble, or perhaps because of it, Miss Mansfield encouraged Jack's writing ability for the first time. He began to give her short stories for her critique outside of school and even began working on a novel, entitled *Jack Kerouac Explores the Merrimack*, scribbled in one of the notebooks that would become a Kerouac trademark. His parents were not pleased with his sudden burst of literary activity. What his father wanted, and expected, was for Jack to explore and develop his athletic ability. Always eager to please his parents (even while at the same time fearing them), Jack did so.

The first evidence of Jack's natural gift of physical prowess was the October 1935 challenge he issued, in a letter to the *Lowell Sun*, to all local 13- to 15-year-olds to come and play against his sandlot football team, the Dracut Tigers. During a game against another neighborhood team, the Rosemont Tigers, Kerouac ran for nine touchdowns. The crowd, including the men at the Pawtucketville Social Club, which Leo Kerouac was managing part-time while looking for more-stable work, raved about the young Kerouac's play in the game. Jealousy spread quickly, and when another team suggested a revenge game against Kerouac's team, he was targeted by the biggest, oldest players and was bloodied and beaten even while still winning the game for his team. The Dracut Tigers became well enough known to spend Saturday mornings traveling from town to town challenging the local teams. Kerouac began to meet the young men whom he would play with and against in just a few years during his own stellar high school football and track career. In turn that success would pave his way to higher education and to meeting the men and women who would become his surrogate family and change him and the face of American letters forever.

Alongside his athleticism, Jack was also fostering his intellectualism, cultivating relationships with the town's creative class. At first making these connections through the theater reviews his father wrote for local papers, Jack soon struck out on his own. He joined a writers' club at the middle school and formed a dramatic group, the Variety Players.

In the friends that he made, he would claim later that he was always looking for a replacement brother, a surrogate Gerard who would not leave him. In Sebastian "Sammy" Sampas, a close friend who saw himself as an actor, Jack found a kindred spirit; a small-town teen who was unafraid to admit to artistic aspirations and with whom Kerouac could spend hours discussing art, theater, and writing.

Sammy was a dramatic young man who thought nothing of jumping on restaurant tables to recite poetry. He carried his affectations, a cigarette holder and an oversize jacket of his father's worn as a cape, proudly. It was Sammy who introduced Kerouac to two of his most profound literary influences—William Saroyan and Thomas Wolfe. Sammy had attracted around him a group of like-minded young men who called themselves the New Prometheans, and Jack soon fell in with their crowd. Sammy had a large family, and Kerouac, overcoming the animosity that existed between the Greeks and the French Canadians in Lowell, would become friendly with all of them. Stella Sampas, Sammy's older sister, developed a deep crush on Kerouac in high school—even carrying his books home from school for him.

Meanwhile, reeling from the blows dealt to him by his now-failing print shop business, which he would be forced to close in bankruptcy in 1937, Leo implored Jack to quit writing, to not even consider it as a future, and to seek work in the mills. Jack's mother, always the most social-class-conscious member of the family, perhaps because of her own bone-poor upbringing, encouraged Jack to think about college, or running a business, but certainly not about being an artist.

As a junior in high school, Jack began to completely abandon himself to the idea of being a writer. He surrounded himself with books and looked for writers and characters who reflected what he saw and heard on the streets among his football-playing friends, in the hobo jungles along Lowell's riverside, and on his hitchhiking forays into Boston. He lost himself not only in the dime novels and detective magazines of the day but also in Hemingway, H. G. Wells, Goethe, and Saroyan. Especially in

Saroyan and Hemingway, Kerouac saw men like the ones he knew, and he began to learn the skill of writing from the masters. He concentrated not solely on the subject matter but instead on the craft of laying out one perfect word after another to create a book that was as perfect and valuable as a string of pearls.

At the same time, Kerouac met the woman who, later in his life, would become representative of all that he felt was good in small-town life: Mary Carney. As teens, Carney and Kerouac seemed as different as night and day. After meeting her at a dance, Kerouac would walk miles to her house in order to spend time with her—yet he was so shy that it was she who initiated their first kiss. Carney was his first high school sweetheart (although she had already dropped out of school in junior high) and the girl to whom he even rashly proposed marriage. (Ironically, it was she who refused the proposal—claiming that Kerouac was too young.)

But Carney's idea of her future was a steady working railroad brakeman husband with a little cottage and lots of babies. When she realized that Jack didn't see such a life in his future, she began to date other boys as well, which infuriated Kerouac (although his commitment to her had not stopped him from enjoying the attention of a tall, redheaded teen named Peggy Coffey). Eventually Carney, who was by this time dating a much older man, grew tired of Jack's indecision between her and Peggy and told him that she thought they should take some time off from their relationship. Jack was crushed. In fact, he was never a serious part of either girl's life again, although he did keep in touch with Mary via letters and nursed a long unrequited love for her, eventually idealizing her as a chance at true love on which he had missed out.

Kerouac believed that he loved her dearly, and even discussed his affection for her in his first published book, *The Town and the City*, and decades later expanded on the theme in *Maggie Cassidy*, named after the main character, who had been fashioned after Carney.

Still nursing a broken heart, Jack turned his focus back to athletics. He had become a member of the football team as a sophomore, and in 1938, as a senior, after two hard, disappointing years of no-glory plays, he was beginning to come into his own. When a twisting run that led to a last-minute touchdown caught the eye of the Columbia football team, they began to recruit him. And although both his father and mother hoped that he would take the other recruiting offer, only 35 miles away at Boston College, Jack, his mind filled with images of New York City that he had gleaned from the endless movie reels of his youth, knew that Columbia was the place that he wanted to be. Just after his graduation, however, Columbia decided that Jack's skipped sixth-grade year was actually coming back to haunt him—he was too small, too thin, and his grades had fallen dangerously low. To get him ready for the Ivy League, they sent him for a year to develop at another New York City institution, the Horace Mann Prep School.

NOTES

1. Jack Kerouac, *Dr. Sax* (New York: Grove, 1959), p. 17.

2. Jack Kerouac, *Visions of Gerard* (New York: Farrar, Straus, 1963), p. 68.

3. Dennis McNally, *Desolate Angel: Jack Kerouac, the Beat Generation, and America* (New York: DaCapo, 2003), p. 6.

4. Gerald Nicosia, *Memory Babe* (Berkeley: University of California Press, 1994), p. 122.

Chapter 2

HORACE MANN AND COLUMBIA

At Horace Mann, a group of ivy-covered buildings in the north Bronx, Jack quickly settled in, establishing himself as a potential football star and starting a small business writing papers for lazier but more wealthy class-mates at two dollars per essay. He explored the city endlessly, delighting in both the high-cultural life of the jazz bands he took in and the low-life characters—the pimps, prostitutes, and hustlers of Times Square with whom he met, interacted, and soon became obsessed. Yet at heart he was still a small-town boy (a fact that most of his rich schoolmates had already figured out).

At Horace Mann, Kerouac excelled on the football team. In the last game of the 1939 season, Kerouac made a touchdown, a 65-yard run, and punted (his weakness at the game of football) 55 yards. As a result, the sports pages once again featured the name of Kerouac across town. He was rated as one of the best backs ever to play for Horace Mann by the *New York Times* and the *Herald Tribune*.

The powers that be had been correct, and by the next fall, Jack was more than ready to attend Columbia. He was ready, although by no means a starter, for the football team. His grades had improved dramatically, and he joined (although soon quit) the socially elite fraternity Phi Gamma Delta. He also registered for the draft. What would become known as World War II was burning across Europe, and even within the ivory tower of Columbia, the call to arms was beginning to be heard. On the same day, October 16, 1940, that Jack registered for the draft, he was also scheduled to play a football game again Saint Benedict's Prep. During a play, he landed wrong and heard the grating pop of a broken bone. His coach re-

fused to believe him and told him to run it off. Ten days later, an x-ray revealed the break. While Jack was laid up, his grades came in—he had
failed chemistry but, as to be expected, showed a particular aptitude for
literature.

His year there went quickly, and he found himself insisting that his
hometown ex-girlfriend, Mary Carney, show up for the spring formal
dance. Carney was unsure but decided to make the trip to New York for
the dance. It was a mistake—to her eyes, Jack (who had fried his skin red
with a sunlamp in an attempt to have a tan for the dance and was wearing
a borrowed tie and tails) had changed for good. She was intimidated by
what she saw as the more sophisticated girls at the dance who had a more
metropolitan sense of style than she. These girls took every chance to
make catty fun of her, and for Mary, the evening was over before it even
began. She told Jack that she wanted nothing to do with him if he was
planning on staying in New York and even went so far as to tell him that
the city would be the end of him—that his best chance would be to come
home to Lowell, where he could find the home that she felt he missed.
Kerouac refused to come home to Lowell and to think about marriage;
and though he would identify the dance and the decision he made there
as one of the most momentous of his life, he knew there was only one answer for Mary: No.

The school suggested that Kerouac make up his chemistry work over
the summer, and Jack agreed. That summer, though, he ignored the press-
ing need to make up his failed work and spent his time hanging out with
his old Lowell gang, chasing women and drinking beer. He focused on
having adventures and enjoying life. During that summer, he became obsessed with Wolfe's *Look Homeward Angel*, identifying it with his own
small-town life and melodramatic family. He was involved in a violent car
wreck with his friends, and this experience, coupled with a wreck the year
before, so scared him that he said these incidents were the reason for the
ironic fact that the man who wrote *On the Road* and became famous for
the idea of constant motion never learned to drive very well, avoiding it
with a fervor bordering on panic.

Returning to Columbia in the fall to begin football practice, Kerouac
found himself no longer very interested in school. During his first few days
there, he met another student, Henri Cru, who would become a lifelong
acquaintance as well as introduce him to pivotal people in his life. Cru
was a vain young man whom Kerouac had known slightly at Horace
Mann. Raised in Paris, Cru spoke French fluently, undoubtedly a draw for
the Francophile Kerouac. It was Cru who introduced Kerouac to the
woman who would become his first wife, Edith "Edie" Parker.

Meanwhile Kerouac clashed with football coach Lou Little again and again. Kerouac's heart clearly wasn't in the game anymore, and Little (as he had done even when Kerouac had been enthusiastic about the sport) took every chance to humiliate Jack in front of the other players. Finally, one day, Jack had enough and walked off the field, dropping out of school as well. Edie Parker, who had been coming to practices to watch Jack perform, was shocked and disappointed by this man whom she was coming to appreciate as more than a friend carelessly throwing away an education that so few had access to. She turned her attentions elsewhere. Jack's career as a scholar and athlete had ended, and in a very real way, part of his life had come to a close as well.

His time at Columbia—the Columbia of the 1940s, with its strict hemline-length requirements for coeds, with freshmen required to wear beanies, with students who broke college rules subject to paddling—this rah-rah all-American life was now over for Jack. A new chapter, one in which the world would come to know the name Kerouac not for football but for books detailing the wild exploits of Jack and his friends, the Beats, was beginning.

Chapter 3

ON THE SEA AND
ON THE ROAD

Straight from Columbia, Kerouac made a quick tourist trip to Washington, D.C., and then returned to his parents' house. There, under the derisive gaze and words of his father, he went to work at a rubber plant in New Haven making tires. Leo began to beg him to go back to school under the football scholarship, claiming that it was Jack's only chance. Instead he left the family home and went to Hartford, Connecticut, to live in a rooming house and work at a gas station, although he knew nothing about cars. There he wrote and compiled his first collection of stories, which would be published after his death in a collection called *Atop an Underwood*.

Finally, once life on his own had lost a bit of its glamour, in the week after Thanksgiving, he headed back to Lowell, where his parents were moving into a new rental home. On December 11, 1941, the Japanese bombed Pearl Harbor, and like so many other young men, Jack signed up for the Naval Air Force Cadet program. His friends thought it odd that he showed so little enthusiasm or excitement for the future that war held, however. While he was waiting to be called up into the program, he worked for a short time at the *Lowell Sun* as a sportswriter. There Jack would finish the work he had to do by noon and spend the rest of the day working on the beginnings of a novel. While his boss, always seeing him typing away, thought him to be a tireless worker, his fellow journalists found him sullen and withdrawn, since he refused to join in the newsroom chatter and banter. Soon, though, he found that the job lacked the Runyonesque glamour that he expected, and he quit not long after he was hired.

Free from the responsibility of his work at the *Lowell Sun*, Kerouac drifted, first back to Washington, D.C., where he worked on a Pentagon construction crew for about two months. Even though it was wartime, boondoggles continued. Kerouac would not spend his time in Washington working, napping, or drinking with the rest of the crew but would instead buy his own pint of gin or whiskey, tuck it into his back pocket, and spend the day exploring the city. Still darkly good-looking, Jack took full advantage of the sexual freedom that accompanied the war, bringing woman after woman back to his room for one night stands before eventually, in the pattern he would follow throughout his life, he grew homesick and returned to Lowell.

He stayed in his hometown long enough to sign up for the Marine Corps, then changed his mind and signed up, after a night of debauchery, as a scullion in the Merchant Marine. On his first trip, to Greenland, he mostly kept to himself, writing a novel entitled *The Sea Is My Brother*. Kerouac scholar Paul Marion, in his introduction to the selection from *The Sea Is My Brother* that appears in the posthumously published *Atop an Underwood*, writes that Kerouac used the titles *The Sea Is My Brother* and *Merchant Mariner* interchangeably, and that both titles are found in his original, 158-page handwritten manuscript. Kerouac would draw on his Merchant Marine experience for other writing as well, including, according to Marion, "a story called 'An Introvert at Sea,' a novel titled *Two Worlds for a New One*, and a one act play 'The Seaman.' " Kerouac described *The Sea Is My Brother* as "man's simple revolt from society as it is, with the inequalities, frustration, and self-inflicted agonies. Wesley Martin [the main character] loved the sea with a strange, lonely love; the sea is his brother and sentencer. He goes down. The story also of another man [Bill Everhart, a secondary character in the story], in contrast, who escapes society for the sea, but finds the sea a place of terrible loneliness."[1]

In this early text, Kerouac was already developing the character that would become his trademark. He wrote in his notes for the project that the characters are "the vanishing American, the big free by, the American Indian, the last of the pioneers, the last of the hoboes."[2]

The Merchant Marine, although not a proper arm of the American military, was still an incredibly dangerous group to be in during wartime. The United States Coast Guard estimates that 600 ships were sunk in World War II, 845 crew members were killed, over 5,000 were missing, and 37 died as prisoners of war. As a grim side note, Kerouac's ship, the *Dorchester*, was sunk on its next run after Kerouac left. During the sinking, the four chaplains on board pressed their life jackets on others. Hollywood would immortalize the tragedy in the movie *The Sullivans*.

Aboard the *Dorchester*, Kerouac had few friends, and the realization that he could be killed although he had no great desire to harm another person repelled him. In Greenland, his self-described high point of the trip occurred when he traded his football jersey to an Inuit in return for a harpoon. There as well, Kerouac left the ship without permission with another crewmate to go hiking in Greenland's wilderness.

That escapade earned him a punishment in the *Dorchester*'s next port of call, Sydney, Nova Scotia. There he was told to stay on ship instead of enjoying a liberty. Instead he called in a boat to take him ashore, where he drank, danced, pushed a shack into the harbor, and then dragged a group of sailors and prostitutes on a housebreaking spree. Arrested by the Canadian Shore Patrol, he broke out of their jail through a window, drank more, and made it back to the *Dorchester*. Despite his AWOL adventures, his only punishment was the penalty of two days' pay—to Kerouac, it undoubtedly seemed a fine bargain.

When he returned to Boston in October 1942, again at loose ends, he traveled to Lowell for a few days, where he received a telegram from his old Columbia coach. Kerouac was welcome to return, the message said, if he was ready to take the bull by the horns. Kerouac thought he was, but after a few days back at Columbia, he realized that he had changed too much to return and left campus disgusted at its isolation and closed-off nature. He had tasted a bit of life and now wanted more, something that Columbia couldn't provide him. His decision not to play football, or return to Columbia, however, didn't interfere with his enjoying his time in New York City.

When Sammy Sampas came down to visit Jack, the visit turned into an endless debauch that involved Benzedrine, marijuana, prostitutes (both male and female), and being caught up in a riot that forced the two of them to shelter overnight in a tenement stairway. Sampas, who had felt himself worldly in the small town of Lowell, was an appalled observer to Kerouac's antics, refusing to participate and wondering how his friend had changed.

Columbia without football, Kerouac felt, had little to offer him. He loafed, drank, and won Edie Parker back from the Naval Air Force cadets who had replaced him in her heart after he had left Columbia and disillusioned her the first time. In February 1943, tired and frustrated with Columbia, he enlisted in the U.S. Navy.

The navy was a far cry from the Merchant Marine. While the Merchant Marine, carrying a reputation as a liberal organization, guaranteed its mariners, via their contract, time to themselves and an eight-hour workday, the wartime navy was all business. Kerouac found himself unable to abide by the navy discipline and what he saw as petty rules designed to mold a person into an obedient individual capable of sacrificing himself.

He was bored by the 18-year-old recruits talking about their lives back home, and the endless round of cleaning garbage cans. He was angered when a base dentist treated him too roughly, and when the commanding officer caught him smoking one morning and slapped him hard across the face, Jack punched him back just as hard in the face. The rules and the authority were all too much for Kerouac. Later that day he simply left the parade ground, went to the library, and lay down. He tried to convince the base psychiatrist that he was insane, but it didn't work. His father came to visit him, saw through his facade immediately, and praised him for fighting back for what he wanted. His father told him that he was doing the right thing. Sammy Sampas, now part of the Army Medical Corps, came to visit him and left shaken, again unable to understand the man his childhood friend had become.

However, it wasn't until Jack left the mental ward, ran naked across the parade ground where visiting military dignitaries were reviewing the troops, and then was caught with stolen butter knives that he was shipped off to Bethesda Naval Hospital. There he convinced a doctor that he was simply incapable of submitting to military discipline. He was given an honorable discharge in May 1943 for "indifferent character." By June 1943, he was back in the Merchant Marine on the SS *George Weems*, transporting bombs to Liverpool, England.

While on board the *George Weems*, Kerouac continued to work on *The Sea Is My Brother*. He began to codify and explain to himself and to others what he felt his life's project would be, writing that a "long concentration on all the fundamental influences of your life will net a chronological series of events that will be open to use as a novel—for a novel should have a sort of developing continuity if nothing else."[3]

On reaching Liverpool, after a dangerous journey featuring an altercation with the first mate, Kerouac's saving the ship by spotting a mine, and a drunken captain who rammed the pier at the Liverpool dock, Kerouac enjoyed two days' leave. He took the train into the English countryside, drank beer, and engaged the services of prostitutes.

When he returned to the United States, after a journey during which the *George Weems* came under attack by submarine, it was into the arms of Edie Parker, his girlfriend with whom he had reunited in New York City before shipping out on the *George Weems*. Jack was finding in Edie a woman consumed with passion and a desire to live life to the fullest. She was taking art classes and was seeking a new way to live outside of her comfortable upper-class midwestern upbringing.

Parker is a difficult figure to pin down. Her relationship with Jack was almost as brother and sister, less sexual than it was platonic. She plays a minor role in Ann Charters's groundbreaking biography of Kerouac, where readers never learn much about Edie's personality. In *Minor Characters*, the memoir of Joyce Johnson, Kerouac's second wife creates a condescending picture of Edie as a rich girl slumming, sowing a few wild oats before planning on settling down with Kerouac and raising a family à la Mary Carney (it is important to note, though, that Johnson admits that she never met Parker). Jack, though, was sweetly fond of Edie, calling her in *The Vanity of Duluoz*, "radiant and happy . . . and young and she was the wife of my youth."[4] At the end of his life, Edie was one of the few people who would still accept his drunken long-distance phone calls, and at his funeral, when people would ask who she was, she would announce proudly, "I'm Mrs. Jack Kerouac!" Their bond, though tumultuous, was to be lifelong.

At this point, Parker lived in Manhattan, where she shared an apartment with Joan Vollmer, and had become a wheel around which people revolved. Kerouac shared an apartment with the two women, and within two months after he moved in, Parker announced that she was pregnant. Kerouac was upset and confused, and before his impending fatherhood had a chance to sink in, Edie had an abortion. Kerouac, at this point still a devout Catholic, was furious at her, and their relationship changed for good. He became less and less interested in her, outside of the occasional sexual encounter and warm bed in which to sleep.

At the same time, the bonds between Kerouac and the people to whom Edie had introduced him were growing stronger. Kerouac immediately took to Edie's friend Allen Ginsberg, discussing Dostoyevsky and art with him. Although Ginsberg would later become synonymous worldwide with poetry, rebellion, and the counterculture, in 1944 he was not much to look at. He was short, with thick glasses and jug handle ears, and was just beginning to realize that he was homosexual. He was dying for a connection to people, especially those who valued the intellect as much as he did. He came to meet Jack at the apartment one morning, and they discovered that they had much in common. They both felt out of place no matter where they were—ghostly, as if they were silent, invisible observers of all that was around them. Eventually Ginsberg would be kicked out of Columbia, which he was attending when Kerouac first met him, unofficially for his homosexual leanings and officially for writing obscenities on his dorm room window. By that time, Ginsberg had timidly confessed his crush on Jack. Kerouac groaned disgustedly but, especially since his own sexual identity was fluid, didn't feel threatened by the unrequited attraction.

Edie also introduced Kerouac to Lucien Carr. One night in June 1944, she convinced Jack to meet a group of her friends, including Carr. Kerouac immediately took to Carr, and they soon became close friends. Carr was the child of rich Saint Louis parents. A student at Columbia, Carr spent his time carousing, much of the time with Kerouac in tow. Lucien had already been kicked out of two colleges by the time he met Kerouac, but their antics together were mostly childish fun—getting drunk and rolling each other down streets in empty barrels, for instance. But however innocent Lucien may have seemed at the time, he had a darker side.

Lucien sent William S. Burroughs, another socially prominent but socially deviant Saint Louisan, to meet Kerouac. At age 30, a Harvard graduate and former medical student, Burroughs had involved himself with petty crime and the beginnings of a heroin addiction that would last for decades. Burroughs, who would become one of the most experimental of the Beat writers and gain international notoriety for his book *Naked Lunch*, was at the time doing odd jobs—bartender, exterminator—living off those paychecks and a small trust fund check that came every month. He was fascinated by the underworld and made small-time deals for machine guns and morphine before graduating to bigger and more horrible crimes, including killing his wife, later in his life. Burroughs began to introduce Kerouac to members of the underworld as well as funneling Kerouac's interest in reading to philosophers like Spengler. Carr, Kerouac, Ginsberg, and Parker would gather at Burroughs's apartment for meals, drug experimentation, discussion of literature, and general rowdiness.

Carr's dark past also revealed himself when a red-bearded stranger insinuated himself into their group. David Kammerer was a man obsessed with Carr beyond the point of no return. When Carr had been 14 years old and living in Saint Louis, Kammerer had been his gym teacher and had fallen deeply in love with Carr. Kammerer came from a wealthy family but sacrificed everything—his job, his ties with family, every shred of dignity—to follow Carr around. He traveled across the country to New York City to press on Carr his unwanted attentions. Kammerer's obsessional madness made the group uncomfortable, but he continued to turn up, as if by magic, everywhere they would gather.

Finally, on the morning of August 14, Carr showed up at Kerouac's, pale and shaking. Carr admitted that the night before, when Kammerer had tracked him down once again, to stare obsessively at him, to beg scraps of his clothing, and, Carr claimed, to try to rape him when they wandered into a secluded park, Carr had killed him. He told Kerouac that he had stabbed Kammerer to death with a penknife, tied his hands and feet with shoelaces, tied rocks to the body with pieces of his shirt, and pushed the body into the Hudson River. He had failed to attach enough weight, however, and the Coast Guard would later retrieve the body.

Kerouac calmed his friend down. They went for a walk and dumped Kammerer's glasses, which Carr still had with him, into the sewer. They went to the Metropolitan Museum of Art, where they looked at paintings, and saw a movie. Finally Carr went to his aunt's house, where he called the family's lawyer.

After Carr tuned himself in, Kerouac was arrested the next day as a material witness. Desperate after a week in jail, and his father's refusal to pay the $100 bond, Kerouac called Edie and proposed marriage, so that she would have a better chance of being able to borrow the money from her parents. In the company of a cop, Kerouac and Edie were married, and Kerouac was returned to his cell. On August 30, after Carr has been indicted on second-degree murder, Edie's parents came through with the $2,500 bail, and Kerouac walked out of jail, headed for his new in-laws' house in Grosse Pointe, Michigan. Lucien Carr pleaded guilty to manslaughter and spent a little more than 2 years of a 21-year sentence before being released on parole. Kerouac and his circle were shocked. They had expected Carr to receive probation.

Grosse Pointe was a new world for Kerouac, where he was living in the splendor that he knew his Horace Mann classmates had come from. Butlers and fine furnishings filled the home, and Parker's family adored Kerouac. He went to the library every day and resumed his writing with the goal of becoming a great author. Kerouac kept to himself, which annoyed Edie, who wanted to show him off to her old circle of friends who still lived in Grosse Pointe.

Eventually Jack found a bar to hang out at and spent a good deal of every day sleeping. But he felt out of place and confined by the wealth, and after two months in Grosse Pointe, working in a ball bearing factory, Kerouac had paid his in-laws back. He headed back to New York to ship out as a merchant marine again. He told Edie that they should view this as a separation, and although she accepted it, Parker's family was hurt that it took Kerouac two months to send them a letter saying that he had made his trip to New York City safely.

In New York City, he signed on board the SS *Robert Treat Paine*. However, after a disagreement with the boatswain (a man whom Gerald Nicosia describes as a "230 pound homosexual" who had an eye for Jack),[5] Kerouac jumped ship in Norfolk and returned to New York. This time, however, the Merchant Marine didn't look as kindly on his AWOL behavior as they had during his drunken spree in Nova Scotia. He was forbidden from working with the Merchant Marine for a year, and even after that, he felt as though he had been blacklisted within the service.

Back in Manhattan, Kerouac fell in once again with William Burroughs and the old crowd. Burroughs presented him with a long reading list including Freud, Nietzsche, and Goethe. From these and other books, Kerouac made elaborate notes and spent hours with Burroughs discussing the ideas that sprang into his head from his readings.

In late December 1944, Edie moved back to New York as well, and both she and Jack moved in with Joan Vollmer. A few weeks earlier, Edie's parents had called Jack to tell him that she had been in an auto accident. Kerouac took the train back to Grosse Pointe, fearing that Edie had died. She hadn't, although she had been thrown through her automobile's windshield and had received 52 stitches. Kerouac was so grateful to see her alive that on his return to New York, he wrote to her asking her to come back to the city and live with him as man and wife.

The apartment that they lived in was like an early version of what would later come to be known as a commune. It had five bedrooms, and Joan, now with a baby girl, needed the money that boarders would bring in. Jack told Burroughs about the opening, and Burroughs, who had been suffering from extreme loneliness, moved in and quickly fell in love with Joan. Vicki Russell, a hooker with an extensive knowledge of the underworld and drugs, moved in, as did Hal Chase, a tall, handsome, rawboned guy from Denver who quickly became close friends with Jack. In addition, Ginsberg had begun spending almost all his free time in the apartment, as well.

The happiness was short-lived. By January, Edie had come to realize that she and Jack were not compatible as husband and wife, that Jack was not upset by the crushing poverty in which they lived, and she fled back to the safety of her parents in Michigan. She requested and received an annulment a year later. She continued intermittently to write to Ginsberg, but after their parting, Edie would have no contact with Kerouac for several years.

NOTES

1. Jack Kerouac, *Atop an Underwood* (New York: Viking, 1999), p. 206.

2. Kerouac, *Atop an Underwood*, p. 206.

3. Kerouac, *Atop an Underwood*, p. 206.

4. Jack Kerouac, *The Vanity of Duluoz* (New York: Penguin, 1994), p. 148.

5. Gerald Nicosia, *Memory Babe* (Berkeley: University of California Press, 1994), p. 133.

Chapter 4

BEBOP AND BENZEDRINE

While Jack continued his flirtation with the underworld of nonmainstream sex and drug use, he and his friends also discovered bop music. It's easy to see why Kerouac and so many of the other Beats felt an immediate, visceral attraction to bebop jazz. Bop was faster than the big-band-style jazz that had been popular before bop came into vogue. It was an African American–created form, as jazz had originally been. Musicians who were dissatisfied that jazz had been co-opted, cleaned up, and then played and sold to predominantly white audiences took the music back with bop. Musicians like Kenny Clarke, Dizzy Gillespie, Bud Powell, Charlie Parker, and Thelonious Monk played with the music, sped it up, intensified the emotion coming out of it, while de-emphasizing rhythm.

Like Kerouac and his friends, the bebop musicians felt as if they didn't belong in mainstream American life. Almost all of the first generation of bop stars were African American, and a good number of them had grown up in poverty. Their music was an act of escape and defiance. The individual took a greater role in this music, unlike the group dynamic that had served as the model in swing jazz. In fact, the extended spontaneous solo is perhaps bop's greatest contribution to jazz, and the solo was one of the main attractions of bebop for Kerouac.

Bop artists also approached their performance in a different way. While the swing artists played up to their audience, the bop artist was "cool," sometimes, as in the case of Miles Davis, even turning his back to the audience. The bop artist played music for the art, not for the audience's enjoyment. The bop artist wanted the audience to come along on the trip, but if they were hesitant, he wasn't waiting for them to catch up.

Stylistically, the bebop revolution was primarily rhythmic. Swing music was built on a four-beat foundation and received texture from the instruments. In bop, artists experimented with rhythmic layering, providing a contact beat through the use of ride cymbals, snare shots, and rim shots. The piano as an instrument took a larger role, playing not only melody but also rhythm.

Just as in Beat literature, many critics accused the new bop musicians of creating music without structure, lacking in discipline, but most tunes were solidly, if not complexly, constructed (as a parallel, witness the furor around the writing of On the Road and Truman Capote's famously catty remark that Kerouac's books weren't examples of writing, only examples of typing). Bop fit into the Beat ideas perfectly because it so closely resembled human speech as it was captured word for word—there were stutters and false stops in bop's dissonance, individuality, creativity, and endless possibility.

In addition, the bop fans developed an entire subculture whose markers—dark glasses, berets, goatees, and drug use—would also come to be identified with the Beats when Kerouac and others wholeheartedly embraced bop music and its outsider status. John Clellon Holmes, a friend of Kerouac and author of the Beat novel Go, remarked that "if a person dug Bop, we knew something about his sex life, his kick in literature and the arts, his attitudes towards joy, violence, Negroes, and the very processes of awareness."[1]

In 1945 Kerouac was also introduced to one of the mainstays of his life, and also one of the factors leading to his later erratic behavior and health problems. Vicki Russell, the towering hooker and member of the Joan Vollmer "commune," taught Jack how to break open asthma inhalers to get at the Benzedrine-soaked cotton and then swallow the wad or soak it in coffee to access the amphetamine.

Although Jack always had a large experimental appetite for drugs, legal and illegal, he took to Benzedrine like no other. Jack relied on the drug, and it became so identified with his writing and his talent that it eventually became identified not only with him specifically but also with the entire Beat movement.

At the same time, Kerouac's Denver friend Ed White said that by the mid- to late 1940s, Kerouac had seriously begun to question the Catholic faith.[2] Kerouac did not feel that he could reconcile the restriction of the church with his desire to do "bad" things—such as engaging in drug and sexual experimentation. It is without doubt that part of Kerouac always saw the path of the Catholic saint (as seen through the lens of his brother Gerard) as a desirous path to follow, yet at the same time, he felt that it was only in the underworld that he could find the truth about life. White suggests that Kerouac told him that Gerard was able to remain a "saint" because he never had to grow up and face decisions about desire, passion, and needs. Kerouac, although just as obsessed as his dead brother with the path to heaven, had to balance his carnal appetites with his spiritual appetite—a struggle that he was never able to fully overcome and one that tormented him throughout his adult life.

In 1946, in the midst of all these starts in Kerouac's life, he had two sudden stops. The first came when he was hospitalized after his legs swelled from thrombosis brought on by a steady diet of alcohol, Benzedrine, and little sleep. The second came when he left the VA hospital and headed straight to his parents' new home in Ozone Park, New York, where he found his father dying from stomach cancer. When Leo died in May 1946, he made his son swear that he would take care of Gabrielle. Kerouac swore that he would. Ironically, after his father was buried and Jack and Gabrielle returned to Ozone Park, it was Gabrielle who took a job in a shoe factory while Jack sat down to work on his first "real" novel, a fictionalized autobiography, originally entitled *Galloway*, which would be published as *The Town and the City*.

NOTES

1. Dennis McNally, *Desolate Angel: Jack Kerouac, the Beat Generation, and America* (New York: DaCapo, 2003), p. 42.
2. Gerald Nicosia, *Memory Babe* (Berkeley: University of California Press, 1994), p. 208.

Chapter 5

THE TOWN AND THE CITY

It's easy for readers who are approaching Kerouac for the first time to ig-nore *The Town and the City* and go on to his best-known work, *On the Road*. For too many readers, and critics as well, Kerouac begins and ends with *On the Road*, yet he had already been writing and publishing for years when he produced the seminal Beat text. He was, when he had his drink-ing under control, a man who wrote as easily as he breathed. The intro-duction to *Atop an Underwood* quotes Kerouac's response to the question "What is a born writer?": "When the question is therefore asked, 'Are writers made or born?' one should first ask, 'Do you mean writers with tal-ent or writers with originality?' Because anybody can write, but not every-body invents new forms of writing."[1] Kerouac felt that he had been born to write and saw himself as a transcriber of life without blunting it, spe-cializing in the transcription of honesty.

The Town and the City is a long book, with a plot that spans generations. It received tepid reviews when it was first published, and it has less to do with the wild Beat idea than it does with fitting into a lineage that in-vokes Thomas Wolfe. Yet readers who are interested in understanding Kerouac's themes and methods, as well as his place in American litera-ture, owe it to themselves to start with Kerouac's first published book.

In *The Town and the City*, Kerouac brings forth the ideas that he will work through for the rest of his writing career—dichotomies like the one in the book's title, as well as family and friends, love and lust, and the re-lationship between father and son. All these themes, as well as the novel's pervading sadness, set the stage thematically, if not stylistically, for the rest of his writing career.

And yet there is a nostalgic softness to the book, as well. Even though George and Marge Martin are obviously based on Kerouac's own parents, there is no dead brother. George Martin is a successful businessman rather than a man who moves from job to job without ever really achieving the recognition or success for which Kerouac's father hungered.

The story involves a family of brothers, Joe, Francis (Gerard Kerouac's real first name), and Peter, whose story begins in 1935. Peter Martin is a 13-year-old boy when the book begins. He is confused about what to do with his life. He's athletic and intelligent and uses those attributes to win a scholarship to the University of Pennsylvania. Peter is a prototypical Kerouac hero. He possesses a deep melancholy that is worsened by his inability to express it in ways that others can understand.

The family moves to New York City, and the brothers George and Peter argue over Peter's new friends, who resemble Kerouac's New York City coterie. One of these friends, Junky, a habitué of Times Square, utters the phrase that would soon bring Kerouac both fame and misery. "Don't you know," Junky says, "I'm beat."[2]

With his friends in New York City, Peter listens to jazz and smokes marijuana. With his family at home, he eats big pork chop dinners, working all the while to preserve the dichotomous split between the two.

At the end of the book, after character after character dies, including George, the family moves apart, with no hope of the line continuing. Peter finds himself on a lonely highway on a rainy night. In his mind, he hears the voice of his father carried with the rain, asking him where he is going, but Peter has no answer for his dead father's dreams for him.

The Town and the City was telling in another respect, as well. Kerouac began to move from who he wanted to be to who he was becoming—the man who would eventually die overweight, bitter, and drunk. Following the publication and mostly positive critical reception of *The Town and the City*, Kerouac wrote to author Alan Harrington, relaying the new circumstances of his life, "I am no longer 'beat.' I have money, a career. I am more alone than when I 'lurked' on Times Square at 4 A.M. or hitch-hiked penniless down the highways of the night. It's strange. And yet I was never a 'rebel,' only a happy, sheepish imbecile, open-hearted & silly with joys. And so I remain."[3]

The Town and the City was also the first book where Kerouac would use his impressive powers of concentration. From morning until night, he focused on working on the novel. There was no one to distract him, as all his friends had temporarily left the city. Burroughs had fled a narcotics charge and was living in Texas on a marijuana farm. Vollmer had lost her mind in a Benzedrine-inspired breakdown and had been committed to

Bellevue. Ginsberg had devoted himself almost completely to drugs. For Kerouac, the time of writing *The Town and the City* was the calm before the storm.

NOTES

1. Jack Kerouac, *Atop an Underwood* (New York: Viking, 1999), p. xiii.
2. Jack Kerouac, *The Town and the City* (New York: Harcourt, 1983), p. 279.
3. Jack Kerouac, *Selected Letters, 1940–1956* (New York: Viking, 1995), p. 188.

Chapter 6

NEAL CASSADY

In late 1946, that storm would break with the arrival of a handsome, lithe, muscular westerner named Neal Cassady. A former inmate, Cassady had been introduced by way of letters to Kerouac by Hal Chase, one of Kerouac's friends from the commune. Kerouac had spent long months with Chase, who seemed to Kerouac to embody the American ideal. Chase was intelligent and honest, self-reliant and plainspoken. He and Kerouac would read aloud to each other the pages of James Joyce's *Finnegan's Wake*, entranced by the sound of the language. For his part, Chase couldn't understand why Kerouac spent time with people like Burroughs and Ginsberg, whom Chase saw as being nihilistic, as opposed to enjoying the passion for life that both he and Kerouac shared. Before long, uninterested in the sexual and substance experimentation going on within the nascent Beat culture, Chase drifted away from the scene and went back to Denver in the summer of 1946, but not before he had shown Kerouac and Ginsberg letters that Cassady had written him from reform school.

For Kerouac, Cassady's youth (he was only 20 when he and Kerouac met) and enthusiasm about everything, especially sex, cars, and freedom from the East Coast elitism that had often irritated Jack since his Horace Mann days, struck Kerouac as the American West embodied. In a very real way, Cassady was the other half of Kerouac: the part he believed that he had been in Lowell, the action man, the sexual hero, the man who played by no one's rules and didn't worry about helping or taking care of anyone. Cassady and Kerouac spent their evenings engaged in long talks until, finally, Cassady asked him to teach him how to write. Kerouac denied that he could, but the moment of calculated flattery cemented their friendship.

In truth, Cassady's life had been anything but romantic. The child of a wino, Cassady had grown up in flophouses and at age 14 began stealing cars. According to McNally in *Desolate Angel*, "By the age of 21, he had stolen 500 cars, been arrested ten times, convicted six times and spent fifteen months in jail."[1] Cassady spent the summer talking with Jack, while Ginsberg fell in love with Cassady.

At the same time, Cassady's teenage wife, LuAnn, had grown tired of the small New Jersey apartment and had been fired for stealing money from her cashier's job (at Cassady's suggestion). In her quest to get away, LuAnn lied to Cassady (who had a deep fear of authority figures resulting from his reform school days), telling him that a policeman had come by the apartment looking for him. Cassady fled in terror for three days. During that time, LuAnn packed her belongings and headed back to Denver via Greyhound. Cassady stayed for a few more months, working at a parking lot, before finally deciding to head back west to find his errant wife. In March 1947, when Cassady finally left on the bus, Ginsberg and Kerouac promised to follow soon after. In the meantime, Jack and Neal began one of the great correspondences in American letters. Cassady sent Jack long letters detailing his escapades. Finally, as promised, and spurred on by Cassady's letters, Kerouac decided to leave Ozone Park and head out to meet Cassady and his fate in the West.

As detailed in Kerouac's thinly fictionalized version in his seminal book *On the Road*, the trip started out poorly. Jack dressed poorly for the deserts of the American West where he was heading; he was wearing huarache sandals, part of the New York City hipster uniform of the time, but hardly a good choice for hard traveling. Deciding to take the scenic route—traveling the entire way on U.S. Route 6, which stretches from Cape Cod to Nevada—Kerouac found himself standing in the rain in Bear Mountain, New York. Demoralized, he took a ride back to New York City and then took a bus to Chicago—the first of many miscues and circuitous routes that would plague the trip and, in a larger sense, Kerouac's life overall. In Chicago the trip, as relayed in *On the Road*, took off when he started getting rides with truckers. He was transfixed by the experience of crossing the Mississippi, and a long last drive across the plains with a load of hoboes riding in the back of a truck driven by two midwesterners headed to California. Finally he arrived in Denver just in time to take in the depressing spectacle of Wild West Week. Here Jack tried and failed to pick up girls and then finally began hitchhiking to Denver. Once in Denver, he quickly met up with Neal, Neal's wife LuAnn, his girlfriend Carolyn, and Allen Ginsberg, who had headed out west via bus before Jack had set out via thumb.

In Denver, however, all the thrum and thrill of the parties and the late-night talking meant that Jack and Neal had no time to spend alone, to talk as they had in Ozone Park. Ginsberg, as well, was depressed in the city. As a final blow, just weeks after Kerouac arrived in Denver, Cassady and Ginsberg took off for Texas to help harvest Burroughs's marijuana crop. Depressed by the situation and left without friends, Jack contacted his mother and asked her to send him money. He used the cash to buy a bus ticket to San Francisco, where his prep school friend Henry Cru had offered him a place to stay.

In San Francisco, Jack worked as a security guard, but the bleakness of being an authority figure, combined with the tension of living with Cru and his girlfriend on a tiny houseboat, was enough to send him off once again, this time to Los Angeles. On the bus ride there, he met a petite Chicana named Bea Franco. They linked destinies and headed out into the streets of Los Angeles, looking for a cheap hotel room and taking in the sights. Soon out of cash, they hitched to a small town near Bakersfield, California, where they picked up Bea's son. Soon, though, Jack grew tired of relying on picking cotton for money and playing *Grapes of Wrath*, and he took off for the comfort of home, traveling as far as his money would take him, in this case Pittsburgh, via Greyhound.

There are some interesting moments that must be pointed out in Jack's time together with Bea, especially as played out fictionally in *On the Road*. For Kerouac the writer there was always an idealization of the peasant life in his books. Here he believes that he is taking part in the simple life, the life of the downtrodden. Bea/Terry is a migrant farmworker who has been abused by her husband. Her child has been left with her parents—grape pickers as well. However, even though there are times when Sal/Kerouac does seem genuinely concerned for the woman on the whole, the scenes with Sal and Terry break down into racial stereotype over and over again. Even though after a day's work in the field he finds picking cotton to be a terrible, and terribly difficult, job, he remarks that the "Old Negro couple in the field picked cotton with the same God-blessed patience their grandfathers had practiced in antebellum Alabama." He says that the other pickers "thought I was a Mexican, of course; and in a way I am." Yet he never explains in what way he considers himself a Mexican.[2]

Overall, the Terry/Bea episode also emphasizes the uncaring side of Kerouac, especially when faced with just how uncomfortable the life that he so romanticizes can be. Kerouac, no matter how many times he aligned himself with the simple people, the proletariat, was never able to make the connection that he was able to go home, that at a moment's notice his mother would send him the money he needed to return to the East Coast, yet people like Bea were incapable of ever abandoning their "simple" life.

Much has been made, and rightfully so, of the good-bye scene between Sal and Terry in *On the Road*. He writes of his love for her and his child and of his wish to embrace a simple life, but when cotton picking is revealed as the arduous labor it is, and Jack spends his days resting in the barn while Bea and her little boy pick cotton, he says good-bye to her with a "Well, lackadaddy, I'm on the road again."[3] The callous nature of Kerouac as a person is revealed, and the picaresque nature of the book is revealed as well. Bea Franco continued writing Kerouac from her home in Fresno, asking when they would see each other again. There is no record of Kerouac, who was still legally married to Edie Parker at the time, answering the letters.

After returning, Kerouac jumped into writing *The Town and the City*, again seated at his mother's kitchen table. It was slow going, a far cry from the "spontaneous prose" for which he became famous. When he had completed all 1,100 pages of what he called "a perfect Niagara of a novel," he gave the manuscript to Ginsberg. The death of Kerouac's father and the grief and unsettledness he still felt were palpable in his writing. The patriarch of the book, George Martin, is lauded as an American hero who builds up his printing business while traveling from horse race to poker game with a cigar clamped in his teeth. No matter what befalls the family, George's force of will is able to overcome any problems.

Ginsberg was impressed and began telling his old college professor Mark Van Doren, a man who came from a long, impressive line of American writers and intellectuals. Van Doren in turn shared the manuscript with Lionel Trilling, another well-known American intellectual and Columbia professor, and then sent Jack to meet Alfred Kazin, yet another distinguished critic of American literature. Jack was unable to meet with Kazin and so began submitting the manuscript by himself to various publishing houses and collecting rejection letters.

On July 3, 1948, Jack Kerouac was at a Fourth of July party thrown by a friend of Ginsberg's. It was here that Kerouac meet John Clellon Holmes, a tyro writer like himself. Kerouac and Holmes quickly became close friends, spending evenings at Holmes's apartment discussing literature and listening to jazz.

In the fall of 1948, Kerouac cashed in his GI Bill from his time in the Merchant Marine and began taking classes at the New School for Social Research in Manhattan. Here he took Elbert Lenrow's modern novel course and turned out papers detailing Theodore Dreiser and his approach, which Kerouac felt was impartial and journalistic. These ideas were repeated in the lectures he heard in the informal university of Burroughs's apartment, wherein Bill suggested that the only true way to write was with a cold eye for detail and no sentimentality. Influenced by these two mentors, Kerouac began the first draft of what would become *On the Road* in early November 1948. He called his narrator "Ray Smith" (a nom de plume that, although abandoned in *On the Road*, would finally see the light of day in *The Dharma Bums*). By the time he turned the manuscript in as part of one of his creative writing classes at the end of the fall semester, it had swollen to over 32,000 words. After finishing it, though, he put it away and, instead of reworking it, began to make a long list of projects he wished to challenge next.

But on New Year's Eve 1948, everything would change again. Kerouac was with his mother visiting relatives in North Carolina when Neal showed up at the door with LuAnn. Cassady convinced Jack to shuttle Gabrielle back to Ozone Park while they drove wildly and spent days in jazz joints. Cassady got a job parking cars, and once he had some money together, Neal, Jack, and LuAnn set off on the road again. Thus what started as a three-day holiday party turned into a long, wild road trip, back to visit Burroughs, who was now living in Louisiana, having moved from Texas when the police pressure on his marijuana farm had grown too great. Leaving Burroughs on January 28 (after failing to convince him to loan them money), they headed across Texas and into California. When they reached San Francisco, Neal deserted them without a word.

Without money, Kerouac wandered around hungry, finally scrounging together enough money to take a room in a welfare hotel, where he wrote his mother, asking her to send him cash so that he could come home. When she did wire the money, he bought a bus ticket and returned to New York. He was still smarting from Neal's desertion (the first of many to come) when he received a letter from Robert Giroux, editor in chief of Harcourt Brace, accepting the manuscript of *The Town and the City* for publication. Kerouac was given a $1,000 advance on sales. He was ecstatic and believed for the first time that he would be able to live his life simply by writing books.

Kerouac took his money and headed off (with his mother in tow) to a $75-per-month rental home in Westwood, Colorado. There he relaxed, hiked, and wrote long letters to his friends describing his new book in progress, a roman à clef he was already calling *On the Road*. That happy pace didn't last long, however. His mother soon left for the East Coast, unhappy with life in the West. Kerouac didn't have friends in the area, and he found himself incredibly alone and detached. In July 1949 he took a bus to San Francisco to meet up with Neal once again.

Neal was pleased to see him, and in a few short weeks, the men had convinced themselves that it was time for another adventure. Neal left his wife and children a note saying that he wouldn't be back, and they began taking car-service assignments, first a Plymouth, then a huge Cadillac, as they worked their way to Chicago. After taking in the nightlife, they pooled their last few dollars to pay for a ride to Manhattan, where, exhausted by each other's company, they quickly split and didn't talk again for almost a year.

This tight bond, this craving for experience followed by complete disconnect, was a pattern into which Kerouac and Cassady had fallen. It was as if they were using each other. Kerouac needed someone through which to live, someone who could spur him out of his doldrums, and Cassady was always looking for a willing partner. The combination seemed too volatile, however, and time and time again, the fact that they were, in essence, using each other for their own ends, meant that after each man had each gotten what he wanted, they split up for long periods of time.

At home with his mother, Kerouac sat down again to work on the text of *On the Road*. At this point, however, the draft had nothing to do with Neal, instead focusing on an imaginary Denver businessman who was wracked with feelings of guilt and insecurity while embarking on a trip of spiritual searching. While working on the text, Kerouac received two important pieces of mail. One was from Burroughs, who, after fleeing the country on drug charges, had set up house with Joan in Mexico City. Burroughs found Mexico City to be cheap and delightfully lawless. He invited Kerouac to come down and experience the liberation for himself.

The second piece of mail was from Giroux—a telegram informing Kerouac that the proofs for his book were in and ready to be gone over. That news sent Kerouac on a happy note again. He spent his time talking to Holmes about marriage and children, discussing the possibility of renting a large loft to live in with Holmes and his wife and children. This high mood continued until March 1, 1950, when *The Town and the City* rolled off the presses and into the hands of the critics.

At the time, American literature was obsessed with formality and tradition. The novel was still an elitist form, and the study of that art form was deemed one of the few ways to keep the delineation between low and high art intact. Jack, at this time, still straddled that divide. Although he came from a working-class family, he had also received part of an Ivy League education. While he reveled in the rough-and-tumble life of the working man (and woman), he was also well-read and knowledgeable about French and American literature. And even while he was drafting *On the Road*, he had just published his first novel, which unlike the rest of his oeuvre to come was formal and conformist, living up to the expectations of American literature critics.

However, the dichotomy within Jack between his education and his experience had also produced an uneven book. It was as if the two sides of his life were tearing at him. He had neither the patience nor the ability to produce a truly Waspy book, and the critics realized it, but he longed for the positive critical reception and recognition that he would not garner while he was alive.

Overall, reviews for *The Town and the City* were uneven. According to McNally, "*Newsweek* called it, 'almost a major work,' but said, 'the long-winded nonsense of its intellectuals is well-nigh unreadable,' while *The New York Times* found it a 'rough diamond of a book,' but decided that its negative views of the city were 'exaggerated.' Howard Mumford Jones in *Saturday Review* labeled it 'radically deficient in structure and style...time as development is not related.' *The New Yorker* was least kind, terming it 'ponderous, shambling...tiresome.' "[4]

In the meantime, Kerouac's friends were having troubles of their own. When Burroughs was busted for marijuana and fled to Mexico, Ginsberg, then working as an AP copyboy, realized that many of his letters to Burroughs detailing their illicit drug dealings would be found by the police. Panicking, Ginsberg gathered up the notebooks he had in his possession and talked a friend into driving him to a safe place to drop them off. On the way, the car crashed, the notebooks were found, and Ginsberg, pleading insanity, was sentenced to Columbia Psychiatric Institute for observation. Kerouac was insane with paranoia. Believing he would be tarred with the same brush, he convinced his mother to move back west to Denver with him.

The move was ill-fated from the beginning. They were living in a clapboard cottage west of Denver. The roads were dirt or, more often than not because of the heavy rain, mud. Neither Kerouac nor his mother knew how to drive. All of Kerouac's friends had left. While Kerouac worked hauling watermelons, Gabrielle sat in the house and moped. By June the situation came to a head. Gabrielle insisted that she wanted to move home. Jack packed her up on a bus back to the East Coast and stayed in Denver working, carrying watermelons while drafting and redrafting his writing and nursing his wounds from the harsh reviews.

Although Kerouac claimed to his friends that he was untouched by his reviews, he sensed that the time had come to break away from the established intelligentsia, and the way to do so was with his next book. In June 1950, he hit the highway again, planning to spend just a week more in Denver with friends and then take Burroughs up on his invitation to visit Mexico City and see what he could find in the way of inspiration there. What Kerouac first found was Neal, who immediately decided that he and

Kerouac, along with a third friend named Frank Sheperd, should drive to Mexico City together to see Burroughs.

Once in Mexico, they found it to be much as Burroughs had promised. With the strength of the dollar, they found themselves rich and spent their time buying beer and marijuana and visiting the local whores. As they pushed on through the jungle, though, Kerouac became ill with dysentery. Cassady dropped Kerouac off with Burroughs, then immediately turned around and drove back to the United States, pushing the car long and hard until the engine finally gave out in Lake Charles, Louisiana.

When Kerouac recovered in Mexico, he fell deeply into a 15-joint-a-day marijuana habit, supplemented by Burroughs's morphine, and spent his days wandering the neighborhoods of Mexico City, hallucinating. Living with Bill did nothing to rein in Kerouac's sanity. On the run from drug charges in the United States, here in Mexico, Burroughs had virtually unlimited access to the things he had come to love most: drugs, guns, and male prostitutes. Because of this unfettered experimentation, paranoia had begun to deeply affect Burroughs. He rambled on about the existence of a drug that would turn people into insects and said that he was spending his time trying to think like a bug. Joan, his wife, was completely wasted by her addiction to speed. Her once-beautiful face had shrunken, and her teeth and hair had begun to fall out. Her body was covered in open sores.

In Kerouac's journals, he wrote that he had begun to think of himself as a new kind of American saint who had to pay for the sins of the homeland, echoing his identification of his brother as a saint who had to sacrifice himself for the well-being of the Kerouac family. Finally, after attending a bullfight while extremely high, Kerouac was sickened by what he saw as the decadence all around him and decided it was time to go back to America.

Early in the fall of 1950, he returned to the United States with his notebooks and two and a half pounds of marijuana and headed toward the home of his mother to work on the draft of *On the Road*, which had begun to change into a meditation about life on the road and about Neal Cassady, the "holy goof." At the same time, now back in Manhattan, Kerouac became reacquainted with Joan Haverty, the girlfriend of his recently deceased friend Bill Cannastra. Haverty was thin and pretty and trying to escape her upper-class life by living a life she saw as Bohemian. When Kerouac met her, she was working in a department store. When Kerouac came by the apartment and found her there, he asked her out to a party, then to a movie. The next day, Kerouac impulsively asked her to marry him, and she agreed. They were married by a judge on November 17, 1950, in Joan's apartment. The party lasted late into the night.

The marriage worked out well for both of them at first. Joan wanted a reason to stay in New York, and in the beginning, Jack seemed like a proto-typical 1950s husband—headstrong and family minded. Jack believed that his mother would approve and even come to enjoy the company of his new wife. After a few weeks of living alone with Joan, he insisted they move back in with his mother. Joan was a working girl, and Kerouac felt that he needed someone to take care of him. One morning, Jack woke Joan at 5 A.M., telling her that he wanted her to get up and make him a spice cake. When she refused, he replied that his mother would have baked it for him. Once they moved, Gabrielle harassed Joan endlessly about everything from the proper way to make a hot dog to the best way to keep house. In his mother's house, Jack insisted on sleeping in his childhood room. Every morning the couple was awakened by Gabrielle coming into the room to bring "Jackie" his glass of juice. In December, Gabrielle's dislike of Joan (Gabrielle refused to speak in anything but French when Joan was present, to exclude her from conversations) and the complete lack of privacy proved too much for Joan. She moved into a brownstone in Manhattan, and Jack soon followed, angry and reluctant.

Finally, on April 5, 1951, fueled by Benzedrine and coffee, Jack sat down behind a screen with a typewriter fed by a long, continuous sheet of teletype paper and rewrote *On the Road* as the book of Cassady, detailing their trips together since 1947 with a new style that attempted to capture the quickness, rhythm, and repetition of life on the road. Of *On the Road* he said that it was "the first, as the French Canadian novel will be the sec-ond in a series of connected novels revolving around a central plan that eventually will be my life work, a structure of types of people and destinies belonging to this generation and referable to one another in one immense circle of acquaintances."[5]

Kerouac wrote 175,000 words in 20 days but told his friend Holmes that he wasn't sure if it was any good, since he hadn't had any time to read it. The book came with a high price, though: Joan's dissatisfaction with supporting a man who refused not only to work at a traditional job but also to communicate with her in any way. Joan was disillusioned by Jack's reluctance to act like a "real" husband, with a steady job and care for his family. Both of them indulged in extramarital dalliances. When Jack came home and found Joan in bed with another man, he told his friends that he was hurt so badly that he would never marry again. Finally, Joan threw him out of their home on May 5.

He moved back in with his mother at first, and then to the loft of a friend, Lucien Carr, where Kerouac continued to write on his teletype paper for hours. When the novel was finished, few of its readers accepted it. Ginsberg said it was too loose and rambling. Giroux wanted nothing to do with it because of the subject matter. Holmes gave it to his agent, who deemed it unpublishable. A final, shocking blow came to Kerouac a few weeks later when Joan contacted him to tell him that she was pregnant. Jack immediately denied paternity and told her he wanted nothing to do with the child.

Critics have debated this move by Kerouac for years. Some say that it was simply pragmatic, that he had found his new voice and realized that a child would complicate matters by forcing him to get a regular job. Others suggest that he had such a bleak view of the current world situation that he was nobly refusing to take responsibility for bringing another life into an already terrible world. The simplest answer is probably the best, however; Kerouac was selfish. His words and actions throughout his life prove this. Like an adolescent, he craved what he called "kicks" without taking responsibility for his actions. Still living with his mother, he was unwilling to take on the responsibilities of being a man and thus lose his independence and be forced to think of others. Regardless of his wishes, Janet Michelle Kerouac was born on February 16, 1952. Kerouac neither acknowledged her nor provided financial support.

In December 1951, after months of hospitalization for thrombophlebitis, a disease that would plague him throughout his life and send him repeatedly to VA hospitals across America, Kerouac headed by bus to San Pedro, California, to take a job on a cargo ship. When he arrived, however, he found that because he had no seniority within the union, there was no place for him. With his last few dollars, he found his way to San Francisco and the home of Carolyn and Neal Cassady and their three children. Slowly but surely, Kerouac began to fall in love with his friend's wife.

Carolyn Cassady was a contradiction in terms. A well-educated woman with a master's degree, she tolerated Neal's infidelities while remaining a dutiful wife at home, raising the children, and waiting for her husband to return, whether it was from a weeklong job on the railroad where he worked as a brakeman, from a monthlong trip with Kerouac (during which she knew that multiple insistences of adultery, and more often than not bigamy, would occur), or from jail, where Neal, who had grown up in a boys' reformatory, would bounce in and out of for the rest of his life.

The time that Jack spent there was the one of the happiest of his life. In the evenings, Jack and Neal would drink and smoke marijuana and then tape-record their endless, far-reaching conversations, including impromptu jam sessions performed on recorders, flutes, or whatever pots and pans were available. Carolyn wasn't impressed by their conversations. "They thought they were being clever," she later said, "but it was just the drugs."[6] She was pleased that they were all home together, in a strange but happy ménage à trois. They went for walks in the evening as well and from time to time dined out together in inexpensive Chinese restaurants.

While all this turmoil was going on in his life, Kerouac had also begun to try to codify his writing technique, what he was now calling "sketching." Like an artist capturing impressions of the world around him with fast-paced line drawings, Kerouac attempted to sketch his impression of the world around him through a sharply focused, sharply defined point of view.

Meanwhile the manuscript of On the Road was still moving from editor to editor in search of a publisher. When Ginsberg had been arrested for his involvement with Burroughs, he had claimed insanity and had been committed to a state mental institution for a short time. While he was there, he met Carl Solomon, a fellow inmate. Never one to waste a chance for networking, Ginsberg struck up a conversation with the educated young man and found that his uncle was A. A. Wynn, owner of the New York publishing house Ace Books. Ginsberg immediately saw the opportunity and began attempting to sell his friends' books to Ace. Burroughs's autobiography of addiction, Junky, was immediately snapped up. Wynn and Solomon, however, weren't interested in either On the Road or the fragments Ginsberg showed them of a strange new book, Visions of Cody, that Kerouac was working on, calling the excerpts that came their way "unpublishable." Ginsberg went so far as to mock the language: "an't you read what I'm shayinoo im tryinting think try I mea mama thatshokay but you gotta make sense you gotta muk sense, jub, jack, fik, anyone can bup it, you bubblerel, Zagg."[7]

At the same time, tensions arose between John Clellon Holmes and Kerouac when Holmes's book Go, later recognized as the first true Beat novel, was published by Charles Scribner's Sons. Kerouac immediately became jealous and claimed (strangely, since Holmes had already had more success than any of the others) that Holmes was cashing in on the popularity of the "true artists" of the movement—himself, Ginsberg, Cassady (who had yet to write anything), Burroughs, and Herbert Huncke. Go is a much more traditional book than On the Road. In subject, however, it was very similar. A roman à clef like On the Road, Go detailed the events of Cassady's visit to New York City in 1948. In it, Holmes coined the phrase "the Beat generation." The New York Times Magazine asked Holmes for a longer explanation of the phrase, which became the article "This Is the Beat Generation." Holmes, building on Kerouac's ideas of spirituality and mysticism, suggested that the problem the Beats were trying to solve was "essentially a spiritual problem." To Holmes (and to Kerouac), experimentation with drinking and drugs was (as it had been to Blake and Byron and countless other literary figures) a way to open doors, out of a love for life, rather than from a self-destructive impulse. The Beats, Holmes wrote, "drink to 'come down' or to 'get high' not to illustrate anything. Their excursions into drugs or promiscuity come out of curiosity, not disillusionment."[8] In the article, Holmes connected Kerouac with the term, a coupling that would come to plague Kerouac in his later years as he sought respite and a clearer sense of who he was as a writer. The response to the article was overwhelming, with over 400 letters being sent in response to the piece. One was from an old friend, current admirer, and future wife, Stella Sampas, who wrote simply that she hoped Kerouac wouldn't forget his old friends.

The phrase "Beat generation" has itself become a source of controversy. Kerouac always tried to tie it to religion and the word "beatific." Herb Caen, a San Francisco gossip columnist who would seize any opportunity to poke fun at Kerouac, coined the phrase "beatnik" as an insult. Kerouac sought to distance himself from it. In a *New York Herald Tribune* interview, he said, "Listen, I'm a railroad brakeman, merchant marine deckhand in war time. Beatniks don't do those things. They don't want to work. They don't want to get jobs."[9] Decades later, shortly before his death, Kerouac, in a disastrous television interview on William Buckley's *Firing Line*, said that the meaning that "Beat" had come to have had nothing to do with what he saw as the universal, saintly meaning he had attempted to imbue it with. "Being a Catholic," he said, "I believe in order, tenderness, and piety."[10]

While Kerouac stayed in San Francisco with the Cassadys in 1951, he began work on a sprawling, experimental book called *Visions of Cody*, a text that at its core relies on the tape-recorded conversations of Neal and Jack, as banal as they often were, to provide the organizing principle for the rest of the book's flights of fancy. Jack believed that *Visions of Cody* was an "American monologue" in the same way that a Charlie Parker or Lester Young solo was definitive, individual, bending only to its own rules, yet also part of the whole. In March, after feverish work with Neal, Jack finished the manuscript and put it in his backpack.

Visions of Cody was Kerouac's most experimental work so far. Ginsberg called it a more in-depth version of *On the Road* when he first read it. Writing the novel brought Kerouac and Neal closer together than ever before. At times, it seemed to Kerouac as if their personalities were melding. Although for years they had referred to each other as blood brothers, for the first time Kerouac began to list the similarities of their lives. That they were both Catholics was the most important, he decided, and he felt that there was a special aura of confession between them, like parishioner and priest, where it was a sin to hold anything back.

In the book, Jack sees Cassady as an embodiment of the American ideal: he's strong, handsome, and smart, idealistic and romantic with a hint in the back of his mind that he has been betrayed by his country. Kerouac seems, however, to be writing not a straight or true discussion of Cody but rather a vision of himself, Kerouac, as he wished to be. He was creating a new Cassady, regardless of how Neal saw himself. After all, in Cassady's autobiography, *The First Third*, he anguishes over the years of homelessness with his hobo father, while in *Visions of Cody*, Kerouac glosses over this aspect of Cassady's psyche.

The book, like most of Kerouac's work, is split into parts. The first part, like the first part of *On the Road*, details Jack Duluoz's preparations to meet Cody Pomeray, writing him a letter announcing his decision to meet him in San Francisco.

Part 2 focuses on Cody's Denver youth and Duluoz's journey across America to meet him. Immediately Kerouac begins to draw comparisons between the two characters, bringing forth the fact that they both grew up poor in urban centers (the images of red brick and neon play repeated roles in the book) and that they are both rootless and restless, and when they are forced to put down roots, they suffer mercilessly.

Part 3 is Kerouac's transcriptions of the tapes that Cody and their friends made. The voices jump over each other, finishing each other's thoughts and delighting in the wordplay through which they attempt to one-up each other. In the "Imitations of the Tape" section, the text becomes even more complex. In it, Kerouac parodies everything that he has written so far and even other writings as well. He takes on, among other things, the writing that his father did for the *Spotlight*, while playing around with a cacophony of other voices—Twain, Dickens, Yeats, Hemingway, and Christ.

The book, which was one of Kerouac's favorites, is difficult to read because there isn't a standard narrative. So closely involved with the book is he, so personal a text is it, that Kerouac couldn't, or wouldn't, find the distance to create a text that would be more comprehensible to his audience. Kerouac wrote in the preface of the 1957 limited edition of selections from *Visions of Cody*, "I wanted a vertical, metaphysical study of Cody's character and its relationship to the general 'America,' " adding that the book was "based on my belief in the goodness of the hero and his position as an archetypal American Man."[11]

When he started passing the manuscript around, he was reviled for including the tape-recorded transcriptions. Readers felt that Kerouac was being lazy by not translating the raw material into prose. In turn, Kerouac was disappointed that his readers couldn't see his attempt to destroy the linearity of novels, to avoid the dead end, the stopping place that all novels, as linear objects, must have.

At the same time, hunched over the tape recorder, stoned, late into the night, Jack was relaying the story of *Doctor Sax*, a hallucinatory fairy tale that had preyed on his mind since his childhood, beginning shortly after the death of his brother Gerard. *Doctor Sax* (or "St. Sax," as Kerouac was never clear, nor would he choose, what the proper manner of address was) had been bubbling in the back of his mind since 1948. He began to play out the plot in some of his letters to friends.

In a letter to Ginsberg, Kerouac said that within the story he wanted to mix dream, memory, and myth to trace the journey of a young boy into adulthood and maturity. Doctor Sax was a superhero living in Lowell, fighting against the snake of evil that threatened to devour the world. For Kerouac, like so much of his work, it was an autobiography in which memory and dream flowed together like so much hot tar on the macadam streets of his childhood. Within the story were drunken priests, the funerals of children, scrounging for coal, the great flood of 1936, his mother and father, all presided over by an evildoer, Count Condu, who lived in a castle high above the town. His nemesis, Doctor Sax, an alchemist, riverboat pilot, and holy goof like Neal, sought to fight him.

The book is confusing, lapsing into such personal reminiscences that is difficult to find anything resembling a plot, sounding instead like what it is—the stoned reminiscences of a boy-man at home with his friends. Jack would begin writing it in San Francisco with the Cassadys and finish it in Mexico City, where he headed in March 1952 to join William S. Burroughs.

The year 1952 was a difficult one for Kerouac. While his manuscripts bounced from publishing house to publishing house and he relied on the kindness of his mother and friends for financial support, his friends' careers were taking off. John Holmes's *Go* was accepted with an advance so large that he was able to buy a tastefully decorated 14-room Victorian house in Old Saybrook, Connecticut. Renowned poet William Carlos Williams was pushing for Ginsberg's collection of poetry to be published by a major press and telling everyone that Allen was the best new poet to come along in decades. Lucien Carr was not only holding down a respectable job at United Press International but had also recently married the beautiful Francesca Von Hartz.

Meanwhile life at the Cassadys was getting more and more tense. Kerouac began to get jealous of Neal, who he felt had to be the center of attention at all times. He was disappointed when he saw Neal begin to care about money as he worked brutal 16-hour days in the attempt to save up money for a down payment on a house for his family. And Jack was angry when Neal returned home too exhausted to carry on all-night discussions with him.

Cassady, in turn, was getting angry at Jack's refusal to get a job and help with household finances. He was making a simple mistake in thinking that Jack was like him—but Jack didn't want to get a job. He was happy in his attic room in the Cassadys' rented house, where he wrote and read the *Encyclopedia Britannica* and drank Neal's wine and smoked Neal's marijuana. It would be these "supplies" that would lead to the friends' parting ways.

With the family cutting the budget severely so that every penny could go toward the down payment on the house, Neal stopped buying booze and dope. Kerouac was furious. He told Neal that he was making a fool out of himself at parties by focusing the conversation on working on the railroad rather than letting the others talk. Jack likened him to a peasant trying to impress his betters while actually only boring them. Neal was furious that Jack would say these things and told him so. Jack took the occasion to pack his bags and tell Burroughs that he was moving to Mexico City to live with him.

Right until the end, Jack hoped for reconciliation. He was happy when Neal offered to drive him to the border, expecting the drive to Mexico to be another wild time. Instead the Cassadys treated it like a family vacation. Neal replaced the backseat of the car with a mattress. At Neal's own suggestion, Jack and Carolyn rode in the back, on the mattress, while Neal rode up front with the children; yet Neal became more and more sullen and withdrawn as the trip continued. He dropped Jack off at the border in May 1952 and drove off without looking back.

NOTES

1. Dennis McNally, *Desolate Angel: Jack Kerouac, the Beat Generation, and America* (New York: DaCapo, 2003), p. 48.

2. Jack Kerouac, *On the Road* (New York: Penguin, 1976), p. 96.

3. Kerouac, *On the Road*, p. 96.

4. McNally, *Desolate Angel*, p. 163.

5. Jack Kerouac, *Atop an Underwood* (New York: Viking, 1999), p. xv.

6. Carolyn Cassady, *Off the Road* (New York: William Morrow, 1990), p. 69.

7. Jack Kerouac. *Selected Letters 1940–1956*, ed. Ann Chartons (New York Viking, 1995), pp. 373–74.

8. J. C. Holmes, "This Is the Beat Generation," *New York Times*, 16 November 1952, p. 10.

9. Maurice Dolber. "Beat Generation." *New York Herald Tribune Book Review*, 22 September 1957, p. 2.

10. Jack Kerouac, on *Firing Line*, 2 September 1968.

11. Jack Kerouac, preface to *Visions of Cody* (New York: Penguin, 1972).

Chapter 7

THE RAILROAD

From the border, Jack took a bus to Mexico City and while on the trip indulged in cigar-size marijuana joints. He wrote long entries in his notebook and insisted that the Indians read them—believing while high that they could read each other's languages, since he had Indian blood in his veins. On stops he huddled in huts with the natives, smoking opium and agreeing with the Indians who said the time had come for a revolution that would put the land back in the hands of its rightful owners.

The Mexico trip was not Kerouac's most productive. He was either continually stoned on the cheap Mexican marijuana or drunk on tequila. He spent most of his time listening to Burroughs, who had just been acquitted of the murder of his wife Joan. One night at a party, Joan had said, "It's about time for our William Tell act," and placed a glass of gin on her head. Burroughs, an excellent marksman, had pulled out his .38 revolver, shot but missed the glass, hitting Joan in her head, killing her. Bill spent his time avoiding the question of the details of Joan's death and focused his energy on rants about politics, sex, and literature. Burroughs had lost everything—his wife, his children, his boyfriend, and his country. All he had left, it seemed to Kerouac, was drugs and writing. Burroughs spent his time working on a new book in the same vein as *Junky*, which he had tentatively titled *Queer*, at Jack's suggestion. All the while, Burroughs was thinking about where to move next. The police were watching him too closely, and he wanted to start over, maybe in Panama, he thought.

Kerouac went to fiestas and the ballet. He visited the squalid brothels of Mexico City and wrote haranguing letters to John Clellon Holmes, warning him not to write a book about jazz, which Kerouac considered his domain. He made plans to write a long book on the Civil War, which he later abandoned—all a product of his hazy, drug-filled mind. He did find time, though, to continue developing the manuscript of *Doctor Sax*, which he had brought with him from California. Writing hunched over the toilet of Burroughs's apartment building (the only place he could find some peace and quiet, as well as not worry about the smell from his marijuana cigarette alerting the authorities), Kerouac fashioned the character Dr. Sax to resemble Burroughs. Kerouac's biographer Ann Charters sees an echo of *The Wizard of Oz*, a movie that Kerouac saw while in Mexico this time, in the conclusion of *Doctor Sax*. The wizard in the book, after all, is revealed to be a scrawny fake. Gerald Nicosia, meanwhile, sees echoes of the film in the gnomes that guard the castle, "pointing spears alternately at us and then themselves in a little ceremony."[1]

Like *Visions of Cody*, *Doctor Sax* is a nonlinear book, albeit one that is more accessible than *Visions of Cody*. Like so many of Kerouac's works, it is broken into parts or books. In part 1, the aura of death is all around. To escape the deaths of his brother, of friends, of other townspeople, Duluoz turns to preadolescent sex play. Meanwhile the narrator's point of view is in a constant state of flux, and time collapses upon itself repeatedly.

In part 2, "A Gloomy Bookmovie," Kerouac divides the text into scenes, like a movie. This part ends with a "grim voyage south to Rhode Island" to see a sporting event, and Duluoz's mother being called in by her husband to repair the torn fabric on a pool table.

Book 3, "More Ghosts," dwells on Duluoz's confusion and fascination with the disordered meeting place of fantasy and reality. These sections also contain a plethora of in-jokes. The over-the-top Amadeus Baroque is a caricature of Kerouac's friend Alan Ansen. The "dovist" artistic movement discussed is a sharp parody of the way critics were beginning to discuss the Beat movement.

In book 4, "The Night the Man with the Watermelon Died," the narrator is once again gripped by the presence of death, as well as the growing realization in his 13-year-old mind that his parents are mortal, as well.

In book 5, "The Flood," the narrator deals with the effects of a massive flood and uses it as a symbol to reinforce the idea that life and death are part of a continuum. The text this time includes poetry and ends with a moralistic statement that suggests that Americans are miserable because of their preoccupation with preserving democratic illusions through the pursuit of material gain.

In book 6, "The Castle," the narrator is making the final steps toward being an adult. He looks for the answers to life's mysteries in the solid logic of books rather than in the magic of cinema. This was the part that Kerouac most enjoyed reading aloud because of its slapstick nature, its funny voices, its sincere attempt at a sort of 1930s screwball humor. The book ends with Doctor Sax taking on the snake of evil and losing, ending up being transformed into a normal man. The world is saved, though, when a giant black bird appears from nowhere to grab the snake and pull it into the heavens, while Sax announces, "The Universe disposes of its own evil!"

By June 1952, with a draft of *Doctor Sax* finished, the tension in the Burroughs house was unbearable. Cassady, according to Charters, had driven down to Mexico City earlier in the summer to try to make amends. It didn't work. Kerouac and Cassady still circled each other like angry dogs spoiling for a fight. Cassady insisted that he would teach Kerouac how to drive in the notoriously cutthroat Mexico City traffic. Kerouac couldn't get the hang of the clutch and stalled repeatedly while Cassady yelled. Cassady couldn't believe anyone could be so inept with cars and left in a huff.

Jack still had no money, and he and Burroughs had begun to argue over what food belonged to whom. Kerouac was down to 158 pounds and looked skeletal. Jack insisted on smoking marijuana in the house during a time when Mexican police were cracking down on expatriates with habits. Burroughs began working on Kerouac's paranoia in the hopes of driving him out of the apartment, spinning wild stories about the malaria, the jungle, and wild animals. Finally, with a final flourish of chutzpah, Kerouac asked Burroughs for $20 for bus fare back to New York City. Burroughs was displeased by the request but gave him the money nonetheless.

After some time in Manhattan, Kerouac made his way down to Rocky Mount, North Carolina, where his mother was living with his sister. Again, Kerouac found a tense household. None too pleased to see him, his sister criticized him constantly for not getting a job, and his mother harangued him about his friends, especially Ginsberg, as her anti-Semitism bubbled to the surface. When a letter arrived from Neal and Carolyn inviting Jack to their new home in San Jose, he took them up on the offer. When Neal heard that Jack was coming out, he was so excited that he sent him a pass to ride the rails for free. Kerouac declined, deciding instead to hitchhike out.

While he was there, things took a turn for the worse. Neal had promised him a job as a brakeman on the Southern Pacific, but once there, Kerouac was shy and awkward and got irritated easily when Neal and the other railroad workers gave the newcomer a bit of a hazing. Jack, who was just starting to feel warm toward Neal again, began to chew on his resentment, ignoring Neal when possible and pouring out his heart to Carolyn Cassady instead.

His crush on Carolyn Cassady blossomed into what he considered full-blown love. They had quiet dinners together while Neal was at work and slipped into bed with each other. Accordingly, Jack's jealousy soon blossomed. Neal, Jack began to think, was too much of a philistine for Carolyn, didn't treat her right, and cared only about himself.

Kerouac continued to withdraw from conversation with Neal, and Neal responded with his own anger, accusing Jack (curiously enough, like Burroughs) of eating more than his fair share of the household food. Jack left in a huff for San Francisco and a welfare hotel to continue his job on the Southern Pacific Railroad—a job whose tips and techniques he had picked up from his once-close friend Cassady.

It was hard, tedious, and dangerous work. Kerouac put himself on a strict schedule, allowing himself margins so tight that he occasionally had to sprint for the trains. He tried to save as much money as possible. When the job took him on overnight trips, he saved money by sleeping outside with the hoboes rather than in the workers' dormitory. For lunch, he ate cheese and crackers, and he cooked toast in his flophouse room with a piece of wire and a hot plate. He was living on no more than two dollars a day, and to him, it seemed like a wonderful adventure.

Soon, though, Kerouac came to know his stretch of track extremely well, so much so, in fact, that he was able to use much of his time to work on a manuscript he was calling *October in the Railroad Earth.*

The book itself was speed-written like so many other of Kerouac's stories. In his sketching style, it tells the tale of his life on the railroad, his skid row room, his sprints for trains, his fear of the rats that scuttled across the San Francisco stockyard platforms, his scrounging for the perfect piece of wire to cook his breakfast on, and his waiting, with frozen hands chapped by the cold metal, to find another pair of gloves to replace the ones he had lost. He worked on what had become his specialty—capturing the rhythms and speech of the railroad workers, and hoboes and people he met along the way.

Every night he would take the notes that he had scribbled down during the day, return to his room and write, with winos fighting and vomiting in the hallways and with the light and street sounds trickling up through his window. He said it was as if he was being attacked by words. He would write until he had exhausted himself, then fall into a deep sleep, only to start it all over again in the morning.

Finally, one day in November, as Kerouac napped on a ratty couch in the employees' lounge in San Jose, he woke up to find Cassady leaning over him, shaking him awake. Neal had a big smile on his face and immediately began to try to talk Kerouac into moving back into the Cassady household. It didn't take much convincing—November was cold and damp, and Kerouac, as always, had a big heart.

When he was finally laid off in early December, it seemed to him to be a blessing, and he packed up again. Originally he planned to head to Mexico and even talked Cassady into driving him. There Jack found that everything had changed. Cassady left as soon as possible after scoring two pounds of marijuana. Burroughs had skipped bail, and for the first time, Kerouac found himself alone in Mexico City. Lonely and depressed, he dreamed of making a new life for himself there with Carolyn, but he abandoned the idea and hitchhiked back to New York City, where his mother was living again.

Christmas 1952 found Kerouac back in New York City and lonely. As an expression of his loneliness and his confusion about his emotions regarding Carolyn, Kerouac began to work on a sketch of his first high school love, which at the time he was calling "Mary Carney." At his mother's home, he wrote, drank, listened to the radio, and smoked opium. He revised the book he had written while working on the railroad. This relived peace didn't last long.

While in New York, he was rootless, aimless, angry at himself and others. He lashed out at everyone with whom he came into contact. He attempted to get *On the Road* published, meeting with agent Malcolm Cowley, but felt that no progress had been made. When Burroughs, through Ginsberg, asked for a blurb for the book jacket of *Junky*, Kerouac refused angrily and told Ginsberg that any such requests should be transmitted not through Allen but through Kerouac's newly retained agent.

By February 1953, a new side of Kerouac's personality had started to show itself. When John Clellon Holmes attempted a conversation with him, Kerouac told Holmes that he was nothing but a rich man out of touch with the Beats, accusing him of ulterior motives in sending Kerouac a gift of $50. While Kerouac was contemplating buying a trailer for his mother, he heard endless stories of the younger Holmes's "mansion." When Kerouac arranged to meet Holmes for a night out and Holmes, held up elsewhere, didn't show up, Kerouac was finished with him, refusing to accept Holmes's note of apology. He wrote Holmes a letter railing against him, saying that if Homes had anything to do with the Beat movement, then Kerouac wanted nothing to do with it, claiming that Holmes had damaged the Kerouac family name by using it in his *New York Times Magazine* Beat generation article. He berated Holmes for coming, as Jack saw it, from a life of privilege, whereas Jack saw himself as a working man. Kerouac went on, childishly claiming that he had never been Holmes's friend but had only come to know him because they lived in the same city.

Holmes was stunned and attempted reconciliation. Kerouac refused and would not answer Holmes's letters for two years. Kerouac drank more and more, preferring Tokay wine and scotch. He was trapped by feelings of insecurity and endlessly bemoaned his emasculation in not being able to earn enough at writing to take care of his mother.

When Ginsberg wrote a blurb for Burroughs's book *Junky* that linked the names of Burroughs and Kerouac, Jack blew up, writing Allen to tell him that not only did he think Ginsberg was too entrenched in the American middle class to ever be the writer he wanted to be but that Jack didn't want the Kerouac name linked to habit-forming drugs.

He wrote long, rambling letters to Carolyn Cassady, suggesting that he was thinking of moving to Canada to work on the railroad there, telling her that he missed her, that he felt his mind was rotting in the city, and that his one great goal, the only thing he thought could save him, was a long stint, alone, in the American wilderness.

In New York, he continued with his old conundrum. He desperately wanted to see *On The Road*, *Visions of Cody*, and *Doctor Sax* published. But when he was drunk, which was most of the time, he was too incapacitated to try to sell any of his work, and when he was (rarely) sober, he was much too shy to approach anyone.

Finally he decided it was time to try something different. For Kerouac, that meant a change of venue, and in May 1953 he once again ended up in San Jose, with plans to work as a brakeman. Kerouac signed on with a crack crew run by a man who pushed his men doubly hard so that they could get a full day's work done in a half day, leaving them more time to themselves. Kerouac showed up, was clumsy and apprehensive, and inexplicably insisted on speaking in French. The crew chief ordered him to sit outside the caboose to keep him out of the way, and humiliated, Kerouac quit.

Meanwhile Neal had fallen on hard times as well. In an attempt to stop a rolling train, he had leaped aboard a boxcar and then was thrown from it, shattering his ankle. Neal wanted Jack to stay with them, but Kerouac, still nursing his crush on Carolyn, found the household to be wildly different when all three of them were unemployed and around the house all day. Kerouac moved back to his skid row hotel.

With no Carolyn and no job, Kerouac had no reason to stay in California, so he signed up as a waiter on the SS *William Carruth*, a ship bound for Alabama, New York, and Korea. At this job, too, he failed. The officers found him aloof and were uncomfortable around him. He spent his nights drinking, and when the *William Carruth* docked in Mobile, Kerouac jumped ship to spend the day carousing half naked with a prostitute.

When he was apprehended and sent back to the ship, he agreed to leave when they stopped in New Orleans. He left with $300 in pay and enough material to write "Slobs of the Kitchen Sea," which was collected with other essays and short stories in his book *Lonesome Traveler*. By August 1953, he was back in New York and at odds with himself again.

NOTE

1. Gerald Nicosia, *Memory Babe* (Berkeley: University of California Press, 1994), p. 408.

Chapter 8

THE SUBTERRANEANS AND SPONTANEOUS PROSE

One of the few productive things that happened to Kerouac during this 1953 sojourn in Manhattan was that he fell in love with a woman named Alene Lee. Half American Indian and half African American, she was a regular among the bohemian scene in Greenwich Village. Kerouac captured their brief, tempestuous relationship in his book *The Subterraneans*, but the very thing that drew him to her—her "exoticism"—that is, her non-Anglo looks and background, also served as their undoing when Kerouac's virulently racist mother found out about the relationship. In retrospect, it's easy to see that a 31-year-old man should have been able to rise above the disapproval of his mother to stay with the woman whom he said he loved, but this episode also spells out the depth and strangeness of the attachment Kerouac had to his mother. It's as if had he broken away from his mother, he would also have had to assume the other trappings of manhood. The same opportunity he had squandered to do the right thing and support his daughter, he passed by here as well, leaving Lee because of his mother's racism.

Instead Lee fell into the arms of Gregory Corso, a young con man with artistic aspirations who had just gotten out of one of his many stints in jail. With Lee in Corso's arms, Kerouac wanted her back immediately. When Ginsberg threw a party for John Clellon Holmes, knowing that Corso and Lee would be attending as a couple, Kerouac spent the night on a raging drunk, crying self-pityingly, then going home to spend three days high on Benzedrine typing out his version of their affair, which he titled *The Subterraneans*, in which he gives the Lee character the name "Mardou Fox.". He spilled it all out, including his fear of her sexuality, his thoughts interpolated with what he saw as the facts of the affair, and ended the story with "And I go home, having lost her love, and write this book."[1]

Also telling is that at the end of the book, Percepied returns to his mother, a theme that winds its way through all Kerouac's work, but never as in this book with the rejection of erotic love for maternal love. Obviously this sets up a rich banquet for the Freudian theory of the Oedipus complex. And even though Freudian criticism has fallen out of favor with today's literary critics, it's difficult to read sections like the one in which Kerouac tries to justify his ill treatment of Lee by suggesting that he is afraid of being left alone and suddenly has a vision of his mother, who speaks to him, saying, "Poor Little Leo, poor Little Leo, you suffer, men suffer so, you're all alone in the world I'll take care of you. I would very much like to take care of you all your days my angel,"[2] and not see some confusion in the dichotomy of romantic and maternal love and caring.

With its interracial plot, *The Subterraneans* was controversial at the time, published a year before the Supreme Court voted to desegregate schools and 10 years before the Civil Rights Act. Indeed, because of the novel's frank description of sexuality, it faced obscenity charges when published in Italy and in America was pushed from publisher to publisher for six years, in part because of its casual surface acceptance of miscegenation. The narrator, Leo Percepied (a pun on "pierced foot," which has been variously interpreted as a Christ image, a reference to Saint Sebastian, and a sly acknowledgment by Kerouac of his Achilles' heel, that is, his dysfunctional relationships with women), makes clear that he understands that his relationship with his "mixed-blood" girlfriend will alienate him from his family and some of his friends. Yet over and over again, Percepied also makes the same racist and sexist comments, seemingly contradicting himself. He is presented not only as someone who is open-minded enough to consider an interracial relationship during a tumultuous time in American race relations but also as someone who has no problem objectifying Lee and others as sexual creatures, suggesting at one point that the women "owe" him sex, and also as an Anglo who is comfortable throwing around the word "nigger." Indeed, Percepied describes himself as "crudely malely sexual and cannot help myself and have lecherous and so on propensities," adding, "as almost all my male readers are no doubt the same."[3]

Tellingly, when Ann Charters tracked down Alene Lee and asked her how she felt about what had happened, she simply shrugged and said that none of what had happened had really been that important to her. To her, it was a simple summer dalliance; but to a man with a personality like Kerouac's, it was all-encompassing, because he used it to say something about himself and his attitudes and beliefs at that point.

The book is also important because it was the only one of Kerouac's works to be made into a Hollywood movie. People enjoyed it because they could read it not as a call for improved race relations but as a daring exposé of Beat culture. Readers were seduced into buying the paperback by its lurid cover, which promised a glimpse into the socially "off-limits" lives of the Beats.

Years later, when the book was finally published, the press was not kind to it. The poet and vehement Kerouac hater Kenneth Rexroth took the occasion to vent more spleen toward Kerouac, writing in his oft-quoted review: "The story is all about jazz and Negroes. Now there are two things Jack knows nothing about—jazz and Negroes."[4]

After his three-day, speed-fueled writing jag, Jack brought the manuscript to Lee to show her what he had written. Lee had read only small amounts of Jack's earlier work and hadn't liked it, feeling that Kerouac's flowing style unnecessarily complicated the reader's understanding of the text. In addition, she hadn't known that Kerouac was taking notes on their relationship. She was angered and repulsed by the way their sexual relationship was portrayed, especially the passages in which Kerouac described her genitals in grotesque, almost frightening terms. She felt that he made her dialogue sound not like her, that he was using the barest details of her, pulling only the worst parts of their relationship and putting words in her mouth. Kerouac was shocked at Lee's anger and offered to destroy the manuscript (although Lee later told biographers that she didn't believe it was the only copy). She refused the gesture, but Kerouac was shaken and worried that when the time came to publish the manuscript, he would have trouble convincing her to sign a libel waver.

To take his mind off the ugly episode, Kerouac headed to Ginsberg's apartment, where a movable party celebrating Burroughs's recent arrival to New York City and his impending departure to North Africa had settled. Here Kerouac showed the assembled crowd the manuscript of *The Subterraneans*, and Ginsberg's and Burroughs's questions about Kerouac's technique led him to write one of the most influential documents of the Beat era, "Essentials of Spontaneous Prose." Before he did so, however, he spent time with the group, completely roiled on wine, speed, tranquilizers, and marijuana, delivering written and oral rants against homosexual writers, including Bowles, McCullers, and Gore Vidal (whom, strangely enough, Kerouac would later proposition sexually, only to end up drunkenly impotent). This episode as well delineates part of Kerouac's divided nature: although he would rant endlessly about the evils and moral turpitude of homosexuality, he also flirted and experimented with Ginsberg and Cassady.

While visiting Ginsberg and Burroughs, Kerouac began to expound on
the way he wrote, which he considered the only true way. His friends were
interested to hear what sort of methodology made it possible to write
manuscripts like *The Subterraneans* in only three days. To accommodate
them, Kerouac put into print his aesthetic manifesto.

"Essentials of Spontaneous Prose" was Kerouac's unifying theory.
Within it, he laid out how he felt fiction should be written, even if he
himself did not always play by its rules. The essay also added to the mystique of Kerouac's fervent on-again, off-again style of writing. The essay
includes elements such as, most famously, "METHOD No periods separating sentence-structures already arbitrarily riddled by false colons and
timid usually needless commas—but the vigorous space dash separating
rhetorical breathing (as jazz musician drawing breath between outblown
phrases)—'measure pauses which are the essentials of our speech'—'divi-
sions of the *sounds* we hear'—'time and how to note it down.' (William
Carlos Williams)." An honest assessment of the "Essentials," however,
with statements like "You're a genius all the time" in the "Techniques for
Modern Prose" section, leaves little doubt that even Kerouac wasn't able
to explain what it was he was doing.[5]

After the breakup of the group, Kerouac fell into a deep depression.
Ginsberg was on his way (via Florida, the Caribbean, and South America)
to California to visit the Cassadys. Kerouac was supposed to follow. Instead he moped around Manhattan drunkenly, unable to hold down a job,
reading voraciously, including, importantly, his first introduction, via a
public library book, to Buddhism.

In Buddhism, Kerouac found what he felt was a similar, although more
exotic—and thus to him more attractive—religion to his native and
deeply felt Old World Catholicism. The first law of Buddhism, "All life is
suffering," struck a chord within him. In fact, in time, the two religions
would meld in his mind to become a strange East-West hybrid of mysticism. This discovery of a new world of thought was enough to rouse him
from his doldrums, and he set off for California excited at the opportunity
to tell the Cassadys about what he had found. When he arrived to try living with the Cassadys once again in January 1954, however, Kerouac
found that the Cassadys had also recently come under the spell of a new
religion—the teachings of the "Sleeping Prophet," Edgar Cayce, an
American who blended together mysticism, reincarnation, clairvoyance,
the lost city of Atlantis, and the concept of karma with Christianity.

Still, Kerouac persisted in trying to convert the Cassadys to Buddhism.
He hunted down a copy of *A Buddhist Bible* at the San Jose public library.
He spent his afternoons there, copying down notes for his sometimes-

heated debates with Neal. He read the Vedic hymns and the *Bhagavad-Gita* and others. By the end of the month, he had over 100 pages of typed notes. What was supposed to have been a joyous time together turned ugly as Kerouac and Cassady took to their newfound faiths with fervor, arguing violently about who had embraced the "right" religion. Finally, however, the breaking point was once again food—this time a dispute over who had paid for pork chops—and again Kerouac took off for a welfare hotel.

In the Cameo Hotel, he began working on a new book—a collection of poems entitled *San Francisco Blues*. Kerouac always said that he had written these poems while sitting in rocking chair looking out the window. They are poems about trains and Neal and are sad and lonely, reveling in a fondly remembered past. Eventually *San Francisco Blues* would join other series of poems like *Mexico City Blues* in one largely imagined volume, *The Book of Blues*. Many of his contemporaries hailed this work as Kerouac's best poetry and felt that he was working on a way to represent the musical blues in a strictly literary form.

In them, he limits himself to the page size of his notebook, calling the form "choruses" and suggesting that each chorus functioned the way that the number of bars does in music. While Kerouac sometimes spoke of bop and blues interchangeably, and admittedly his grasp on musical theory and history is a bit shaky at times—he was called to task repeatedly for misidentifying artists—his appreciation is that of an enthusiast rather than a jazz or blues scholar. It is perhaps because of this lack of intellectual responsibility that he is able to more easily see the connection between blues and the music for which it laid a foundation: jazz.

He brooded for a month at the Cameo, and then, in April 1954, he headed back to his mother and New York City via bus. There he embraced solitude, trying to get out of the doldrums into which he had fallen during his stay in the fleabag hotel. He tried to find other work. Using his newly acquired skills, he found employment on Brooklyn's Dock Railroad but had to quit because of another attack of phlebitis. Mostly he studied Buddhism.

Feeling burned by his experiences with the Cassadys, Kerouac embraced Ginsberg (now in California) as his new best friend. Knowing that Ginsberg as well shared a fascination with Asian religions, Kerouac wanted Ginsberg to take him under his wing and tutor him. The letters to Ginsberg during this period are among Kerouac's strangest. Convinced that he already knew almost everything there was to know about Buddhism, yet as always insecure, his letters are by turn wheedling and insulting; they include bits of his Buddhist manuscript *Some of the Dharma*, in which he likens Buddhist enlightenment to heroin and also recounts his boozy Greenwich Village escapades, even though the Buddha forbade his followers to drink.

Meanwhile, Kerouac was so desperate to find a publisher for *On the Road* that he retitled it *The Beat Generation* in the hopes of latching on to some of the publicity garnered by John Clellon Holmes's work. It didn't succeed, and with his mother furious at him for what she saw as his Buddhist blasphemy and his inability to publish his book, he drank and embraced a new dream—of moving to Mexico to sequester himself and become a sort of Buddhist hermit of his own making.

Instead he sat at home with his mother and caused trouble among his acquaintances. He wrote sutras condemning Ginsberg's ideas of love as Western-style lust that needed to be eliminated to achieve Nirvana. He showed his manuscript of *The Subterraneans* to Corso and Lee and then became enraged, nearly breaking into Lee's home when she wouldn't return the manuscript.

In perhaps the most telling episode of Kerouac's loosening grip on reality, he wrote the Cassadys and told them that the pork chop they had fought over (apparently, a chop that Kerouac was still stewing and chewing over in his grudge-filled mind) was an illusion and that they should embrace Buddhism to understand that concept. In time, though, he forgave even the pork chop incident and was writing love letters to his best friend's wife. Carolyn revealed that psychiatrists had recently tested and classified Neal as prepsychotic. Jack replied that all Neal needed was love, but he was most likely too tied into his problems to have any true empathy for others. Still avoiding child support and still failing to find any publishers, Kerouac wrote in his journal that he felt the world "CONSIDER[S] ME A CRIMINAL AND INSANE AND AN IMBECILE, MY SELF-SELF DISAPPOINTED AND ENDLESSLY SAD BECAUSE I'M NOT DOING WHAT I KNEW SHOULD BE DONE A WHOLE YEAR AGO."[6] In March 1954, Kerouac began talking about leaving New York City again, following the plan that had cooked in his mind for a year of drunken debauches and depressions.

NOTES

1. Jack Kerouac, *The Subterraneans* (New York: Grove, 1958), p. 152.
2. Kerouac, *The Subterraneans*, p. 142.
3. Kerouac, *The Subterraneans*, p. 12.

4. Gerald Nicosia, *Memory Babe* (Berkeley: University of California Press, 1994), p. 463.

5. Jack Kerouac, "Essentials of Spontaneous Prose," in *The Portable Beat Reader*, ed. Ann Charters (New York: Penguin, 1992), p. 57.

6. Nicosia, *Memory Babe*, p. 385.

© Bettman/CORBIS

© Bettman/CORBIS

Chapter 9

MEXICO CITY

In April 1954, Jack was back with his mother in Richmond Hill. He was trying to control his drinking and drug use, feeling that his life was spiraling out of control. While he was there, he focused on collecting transcriptions of his dreams in a manuscript he called *Book of Dreams*. He also took his writing down an unexpected course when he began working on a science fiction story called "cityCityCITY."

"cityCityCITY" began as a transcription of one of Kerouac's dreams about a future society faced with the problem of overpopulation, a problem to which the government has provided the solution of centralized technological control over all citizens. Critics have suggested that Kerouac meant the story to be a statement about the Communist witch-hunt led by Senator Joseph McCarthy. Nicosia writes, "Like McCarthy, the character G-92 in 'cityCityCITY' unconscionably destroys innocent people to persecute personal vendettas and to win favor for himself."[1]

In July 1954, Kerouac was tired again of New York. He felt as if his friends had turned against him, that no one understood the new directions he was trying to take his writing with the nonlinear forms of *Visions of Cody* and *Dr. Sax*. He felt that his agent, Sterling Lord, wasn't working hard enough because *On the Road* still hadn't been sold. He began to think about going back to California again, even though he knew that at the moment "his" room in the Cassady house was occupied—by Ginsberg.

Instead, in October 1954, Jack headed to Lowell, ostensibly to take some notes on a book that he was planning, called *Book of Memory*. He wandered drunk around town and even tracked down Mary Carney, who, as surprised as she must have been, nonetheless invited him in to watch television. He decided that he had fallen in love with her all over again. But when he returned the next day, Mary, tipped off by Jack's phone call, had invited all her family members and her boyfriend over. They refused to even ask Jack to sit down. Dejected, humiliated, he wandered off into the Lowell night and went on a two-day drinking binge that ended with him wandering into the church of Saint Jeanne d'Arc, where he saw a statue of the Virgin Mary turn its head to regard him.

All of this added up to Kerouac's feeling, in December 1954, as if he had reached the lowest point of his life. On January 18, 1955, he showed up in court to make public the sentiment that he had always told his friends, and anyone else who asked, that Joan Haverty's daughter was not his. Kerouac was terrified of going to jail for nonpayment of child support and leaving his mother alone. He brought with him *A Buddhist Bible*, his notes, and some other manuscripts, feeling almost certain that he would be put in jail. In a lucky stroke, the judge declared Kerouac medically disabled when Kerouac's lawyer (Allen Ginsberg's brother) Eugene Brooks presented medical proof of Kerouac's phlebitis. His case was suspended for a year. Joan was amazed at the condition Jack was in. Strung out from the alcohol and drugs, he looked like a different person than the one with whom she had created a child. She suggested a compromise. She would quit hounding him for child support as long as he agreed never to contact his daughter. A relieved Kerouac agreed immediately.

In February 1955, after the trial, he moved to his sister's home in North Carolina to help take care of his nephew. He wrote apologetic letters to the Cassadys. To Ginsberg he wrote that although he still considered himself the best writer in America today, his greatness would be acknowledged not by the prizes or publications but by the number of Americans he would bring to Buddhism. He had already written a new Buddhism book, *Buddha Tells Us*, a translation of the *Surangama Sutra*, and was a biography of the Buddha. Professionally, he was pleased when his work "Jazz of the Beat Generation" appeared in the journal *New World Writing*, and an *On the Road* excerpt called "The Mexican Girl" showed up in the *Paris Review*, and his short story "cityCityCITY" appeared in the *New American Reader*.

But all was still not well. Kerouac was drinking more and more, spending evenings drunkenly shouting at the television. Although his brother-in-law had hired him (in an uncharacteristic show of kindness) to deliver televisions for his business, Jack fudged delivery after delivery, instead spending his time drinking. His mother, worried about him, came to Rocky Mount to help watch over him.

Kerouac felt trapped. He didn't want Carolyn to see him this way: drunken, debauched. The last time he had been in New York, a new breed of hipsters had spent their time ridiculing him and picking fights with him. In the summer of 1955, fed up with Kerouac's behavior, his brother-in-law asked him when he was planning to leave. Added to this stress, in the familiar pattern, his mother began nagging, and so with a loan (this time from Ginsberg's brother), Kerouac headed off to Mexico City.

Good news in the form of a grant from the National Institute of Arts and Letters greeted him in Mexico City. Living in a tiny adobe room in Burroughs's old building (Burroughs had moved to North Africa by this time), Kerouac spent his time reading Buddhist scripture, smoking marijuana, shooting morphine, and working on the book of poems that would be published decades later as *Mexico City Blues*. His stated claim was that the poems were like "a jazz poet blowing long blues in an afternoon jam session on Sunday." And indeed they do have that endless, serene, drawn-out quality that junkie musicians like Miles Davis and John Coltrane would come to create as "cool" jazz. Some of the entries were merely the transcribed ramblings of junkie and fellow expatriate and former Burroughs roommate Bill Garver.

In the poems, Kerouac still focuses on Buddhism and rails against the ineffectualness of his own writing. Ginsberg claimed later that the work in *Mexico City Blues* proved Kerouac's deep understanding of the Buddhist religion. Gary Snyder wasn't convinced, and even Kerouac, in his later years, would sign the book with a cross under his name, the only book in which he did so, almost as a repudiation of the Buddhist beliefs contained in the poems. Michael McClure avoided the Christian-versus-Buddhist controversy and simply said that *Mexico City Blues* is "the finest long religious poem of the twentieth century."[2]

Garver's narcotics dealer was a slum-dwelling Catholic Indian named Esperanza. While in his drug-induced hazes, Kerouac began nursing a crush on her, writing the tale of a junkie princess and changing her name to the title of the book, *Tristessa*. Kerouac adapted her, as he did so many of his idealized women, to fit his current obsession. When, high on morphine, he called her "ma Dame" in his native French, he believed that it had been spiritual inspiration, writing that the reason he had been led to say it was that he had meant "Damema," what he translated as "mother of Buddhas."

Tristessa is an important Kerouac work that is often overlooked. Its importance lies not in its plot or style but in the fact that it is the first book Kerouac wrote after he discovered Buddhism and began to see the world, his writing, and himself almost exclusively within the confines of his search for Buddhist understanding. In Buddhism, Kerouac found an expansion of the ideas of Spengler that Burroughs had introduced him to so many years ago. Kerouac was drawn to the concept of the Kalpas, or epochs of time that act cyclically. Likewise, in the Buddhist concept of compassion for all living things, he felt a strong echo of what his brother Gerard had taught him so many years ago.

The first part of the book, "Trembling and Chaste," describes a trip made with Tristessa to her home to score some morphine. Her room, decorated with a variety of living animals from a Chihuahua to a dove, as well as with Catholic religious iconography, fascinates the narrator. Part 1 ends with the narrator, although desperate to sleep with Tristessa, deciding that she, like a helpless kitten, is best left alone.

Part 2 details the deterioration of Tristessa as Kerouac found her in October 1956, strung out and crippled by her addiction. The narrator, however, still confesses his undying love for her, even going so far as to say that he would marry her if he was junkie. At times, it's hard not to see *Tristessa* as a warming over of *The Subterraneans* with Buddhist philosophy thrown in for good measure.

Despite finishing part 1 of *Tristessa* by September, Jack had grown weary of his surroundings and set off for San Francisco, in possession of one of Ginsberg's poems that had sparked a passion within him, as well as a huge supply of cheap Mexican marijuana and speed. In Berkeley, Ginsberg was once again providing a bridge between the rough-and-tumble underworld and the staid world of academia. He hosted wild parties at his cottage that brought traditionalist poets together with junkie writers. Ginsberg had met people like writer and Buddhist scholar Gary Snyder at other literary salons like the one hosted by poet Kenneth Rexroth. In California, Kerouac met Neal's new girlfriend Natalie Jackson and began, inexplicably, to gall Rexroth simply by his presence.

NOTES

1. Gerald Nicosia, *Memory Babe* (Berkeley: University of California Press, 1994), p. 463.

2. Nicosia, *Memory Babe*, p. 490.

Chapter 10

THE WEST COAST
REVOLUTION

Ginsberg brought Kerouac to one of Rexroth's parties in late September 1955. There he met two poets who would figure prominently in his life and work—Philip Whalen and Gary Snyder. When Kerouac mentioned some Buddhist texts that he had been reading, he was amazed to hear people at the party pick up on the discussion and talk about Buddhism passionately and knowledgeably. When Kerouac expressed his surprise, Rexroth told him snidely, "Everybody in San Francisco is a Buddhist, Kerouac! Didn't you know that?"[1] Rexroth had been the arbitrator of literary fashion on the West Coast for so long that he expected people to pay him the deference and respect he believed were his due. When Kerouac (ignorant of Rexroth's personality) didn't provide fawning praise of Rexroth's work, the elder poet immediately turned against him.

Kerouac spent much of his time with Ginsberg. It was Kerouac who had suggested the title *Howl* for Ginsberg's famous poem. Building on the visions he had during a peyote trip, Ginsberg carved out a space for himself within the bardic poetic tradition somewhere between Blake and Whitman, proving it during his riotous and now legendary first public reading, an event he organized on October 13, 1955, at the Six Gallery in San Francisco.

Later in 1958, Rexroth would tell Richard Wilbur in *The Nation* that he had watched Kerouac frighten his children at a party at Rexroth's house, where Kerouac had pulled a needle out of pocket and given himself a shot of narcotics. Kerouac refused to be drawn into the public battle and even greeted Rexroth every time he saw him. Rexroth would only turn away, refusing to talk.

At the Six Gallery reading, Kerouac continued to enrage Rexroth by dragging in jugs of wine for the audience to drink, by dancing in the aisles, drumming, and shouting "Go!" as the poets read, although all the other poets appreciated the enthusiastic hijinks.[2] Also at the reading was Kerouac's new Buddhist guide, the American poet of the outdoors, Gary Snyder.

Snyder was a tough-minded and tough-writing West Coast poet whose interest in Buddhism was purer and deeper than Kerouac's. Never lording it over him, however, Snyder helped guide Kerouac in new ways of thinking about Buddhism, encouraging him in his quest to spend some solitary time in the woods, in contemplation. Snyder, having been blacklisted out of the Forest Service for his political beliefs, was preparing to head to Japan to study in a Zen Buddhist monastery when Kerouac met him.

Snyder took Kerouac hiking in the mountains, and as they climbed, they made up haikus. Kerouac found a certain serenity in the exertion of the hike and the simple meal that Snyder cooked on the fire that evening. The next day, however, Kerouac missed summiting, becoming fearful of the wind and the height.

After taking quiet, contemplative mountain hikes with Snyder, Jack turned to wilder times with Cassady. Neal had recently become deeply involved with a new girlfriend, Natalie Jackson. Cassady had convinced Natalie to forge Carolyn's name on a $10,000 security scheme and then took the money to the racetrack, where it was almost immediately lost. The guilt and the fear of prison ate Natalie from the inside out; she lost weight and looked like a skeleton. She attempted to slit her wrists rather than go to jail, but Cassady managed to stop her. When he had to leave to go to work, he asked Kerouac to watch her, to make sure she didn't do anything rash.

Despite his interest in religion, compassion was not Kerouac's strong point. He tried to make Jackson eat something to settle her down, but when she refused, Kerouac lost his temper, yelling at her, telling her to calm down, screaming Buddhist aphorisms at her. Finally, convinced that she would go to prison, Natalie slit her own throat with a piece of glass from a broken skylight and then jumped to her death from her apartment building.

The death shook Kerouac and served as a signal that it was time to go home. Kerouac left San Francisco on a circuitous train-jumping, hitch-hiking, and finally bus journey across America, again back to Nin's home in Rocky Mount, North Carolina, in time for Christmas 1955, back to the house where he had started a year ago.

Shaken, exhausted, and demoralized to be back where he started, in a southern culture of masculinity in which he didn't feel he belonged at all,

Kerouac started, under the heavy influence of marijuana and ampheta-mines, to spend 12 days writing mostly from dusk to dawn on what is per-haps his most personal and most pretentious book, *Visions of Gerard*. The book itself is the tale of the short life and early death of his brother Ger-ard. The text itself continues to beatify Gerard, and details the blessings he left on his family before moving on. Although Kerouac had always written autobiographical work, it appears that even decades after Gerard's death, Kerouac was too close to the subject emotionally to write coher-ently about it.

The language of the book is overblown, as if trying consciously to echo Shakespeare. When *Visions of Gerard* was published years later, readers and critics found it mawkish and uneven (certainly the 1963 edition was not helped by its odd line drawings of an angelic Gerard, big eyed, limbs akimbo, often wearing a cravat and pajamas while talking to the birds on his windowsill), and it is hard not to place some of the blame on the prodigious appetite for drugs, alcohol, and self-destruction that had come to the forefront of Kerouac's life again.

The high point of being home was a letter he received, the fruits of his labor with Gary Snyder. The letter offered Kerouac a job as a fire lookout on Desolation Mountain in Washington State's Mount Baker National Forest. A month later, Kerouac learned that Snyder had a place for them to stay in California while Kerouac waited for his job to start and Snyder waited for his freighter to leave for Japan. Making his way across the coun-try again, in March 1956, via bus and hitchhiking (including a quick, frightening trip across the Mexican border to pick up a large amount of marijuana), Kerouac found himself relatively quickly back in Mill Valley, California.

Snyder's work ethic rubbed off on Kerouac, and while staying there, he focused on meditating and working on four large projects: an autobiogra-phy called *The Duluoz Legend*, a film script, a translation of the Buddhist *Diamond Sutra* entitled *The Scripture of the Golden Eternity* (a text whose original manuscript was lost in California), and a long poem, *Old Angel Midnight*.

Old Angel Midnight is set on Good Friday. The poem languished for years, unpublishable until after Kerouac's death, probably because of its dramatically experimental nature. Kerouac himself said that *Old Angel Midnight* (which was originally called *Old Angel Lucien*, after Lucien Carr) had no real narrative or direction but instead focused on the structure and on capturing a cacophony of sounds.

One of the tasks he accomplished there was working on the translation of Buddhist scripture that Snyder had been encouraging him to complete,

The Scripture of the Golden Eternity. When Kerouac completed it, he began working on what he considered formless automatic-writing doodles. He felt that although he was working in the arena of what he called spontaneous prose, it lacked direction and was going nowhere and would probably never see the light of day. The title, originally *Old Angel Lucien*, came from the fact that he was building, in these automatic-writing sections, on a sketch he had done the previous year attempting to capture Lucien Carr's speech patterns. From there Kerouac began to free-associate with what he had already recorded and continued building from there—without revisions. Michael McClure, who wrote the introduction to *Old Angel Midnight*, likens it to scat singing and to Hindu poetry, to *Finnegan's Wake* and to the Katzenjammer Kids.

When the text was prepared for publication consideration, Carr asked for the title change, and it was at that point when Kerouac began to separate the poem into sections. Critics have suggested that in using the stream-of-consciousness style, Kerouac was indebted to one of his writing heroes—James Joyce, especially the Molly Bloom soliloquy that ends the book *Ulysses*.

On May 15, 1956, after a gigantic picnic party, Gary headed off to Japan. Before he left, though, Snyder warned Kerouac about the amount of wine he had been drinking. His worsening alcoholism had led to yet another falling out with Rexroth when Kerouac had made a drunken pass at Rexroth's young daughter and was thrown out of the party. Rexroth began to explicitly exclude Kerouac from his promotions of younger writers, saying, "He's too drronk [sic] all the time."

When not writing the poem, Kerouac spent his time at his rural cottage owned by the Buddhist McCorkle family, meditating under eucalyptus trees, captivated, as he was by the pine trees in his various homes in Florida, by the sound of the wind in their branches. His shack was bare and empty, and Snyder would stop by and help lead Kerouac through his Zen meditation exercises.

Finally, on June 18, 1956, Jack said good-bye to the owners of the cabin and set off hitching from San Francisco to Washington State. Here he would find the solitude for which he had claimed so many times that he wished. Desolation Mountain is 100 miles from Seattle, 35 miles from the nearest town. There was a boat ride from the ranger station, then a six-mile horseback ride to the mountaintop. Kerouac believed that he was so isolated that he would be able to find God and discover what was "the meaning of all this existence and suffering and going to and fro ..."[3]

But telling those around you that you desire true solitude and actually experiencing it are two different things. After two months on Desolation

Mountain, Kerouac would leave and never go back. He arrived on July 5 and quickly ran through his reading material. He tried to pray but was plagued by nightmares and began to have anxiety attacks. Obsessively he sat up late into the nights wondering how he could have left his mother. He began, against his Buddhist beliefs, to kill the mice that inhabited the cabin. In all fairness, manning a fire lookout cabin is not like taking a simple hike in the woods with friends. Suspended in the sky, you feel as if you are naked in the clouds when thunderstorms roll in, which is also one of the busiest times for fire lookouts, as they watch for lightning strikes that could start fires.

The days passed slowly with nothing to fill them except his simple chores of eating, cleaning, and gathering wood. Worse, although he had planned on doing much writing while separated from the world, he found himself almost unable to do any. He spent two months alone writing a letter to his mother. He was there for 63 days and had almost nothing, in the form of writing, to show for it.

Kerouac had bitten off more than he could chew. The woods themselves can be terrifying for city dwellers. Far from the quiet, sylvan paradise often shown in the popular media, the deep woods are a noisy place where even a foraging chipmunk's movements can sound like a rampaging grizzly. Add to this the fact that Kerouac, a drug user and alcoholic, had not brought any of these sorts of supplies with him and now had to deal with symptoms of withdrawal. It was, by all accounts, a poorly thought-out retreat. For decades, Kerouac had looked to others, to jazz, and to alcohol and drugs to drown out the noises that were inside him, to lose his sense of self. On Desolation Mountain, he was confronted by himself and only himself with no one or nothing there to distract him from self-examination. It was not a pleasant time. The first thing he did after returning was to head immediately to the noise, the hustle, and the booze of Seattle, Washington.

Kerouac drank his fill of port in Seattle and hopped on a bus to San Francisco, where along with other members of the old New York gang, Ginsberg and Ginsberg's lover Peter Orlovsky, Cassady, and Corso had their pictures taken as part of the "San Francisco Poetry Renaissance" for *Mademoiselle* magazine. A little later, the *New York Times Book Review* ran an article called "West Coast Rhythms" highlighting the same group. Kerouac was invited to dinners with more-established writers, where he felt uncomfortable, and after a few weeks of it, he decided to hitchhike to Mexico City again.

By all accounts, despite his worsening alcoholism, Kerouac was in the best shape that he had been in years. He spent two months in Mexico

City, beginning in late September 1956. He was clearheaded and extremely creative, pouring out poems and working on draft manuscripts. In Mexico City he soon settled into his regular routine but was horrified to see the drug peddler who had inspired *Tristessa*. Years of drug addiction had ravaged the beauty Kerouac had seen years earlier, the same way alcohol would tear apart Kerouac's rugged good looks by the time he died. Bizarrely he began to blame himself for her condition, writing that if he had not left her, she could have been saved. Even more bizarre, Kerouac attempted to seduce this shadow of a woman, who wet herself and could take only a few steps before collapsing in the dirt. In his free time, he began to set down his latest experiences on the West Coast, including his sojourn into the wilderness, calling it *Desolation Angels*.

NOTES

1. Gerald Nicosia, *Memory Babe* (Berkeley: University of California Press, 1994), p. 491.

2. Jack Kerouac. *Selected Letters 1940–1956*. (New York: Viking, 1995), p. 524.

3. Nicosia, *Memory Babe*, p. 331.

Chapter 11

AFRICA

On November 7, 1955, Ginsberg, Orlovsky, and Corso showed up in Mexico City. They visited the Aztec temples and smoked marijuana, they went to brothels staffed by adolescent prostitutes, and the newest arrivals brought the news to Jack that the *Evergreen Review* wanted to buy *The Subterraneans* for the price of a penny a word. Jack was tired of traveling, though, and Ginsberg took it upon himself to drag Jack around Mexico and to chide him when he felt that Jack was being too whiny.

After a few weeks, they all piled into a small car and drove to Greenwich Village. Kerouac returned to the States thin and bearded, looking like nothing so much as a rough-and-tumble hobo, but he felt clean and reborn, believing that he had left the depression and his obsession with drugs and Mexican prostitutes behind him. Jack finally got word that Viking Press had decided, almost six years after he had first put the tale down on teletype tape, to publish *On the Road* in the following September. He took trips to Washington, D.C., to visit Gregory Corso at Randall Jarrell's house. Kerouac again got drunk and loud and offended Jarrell and his family. Corso was relived to see him go. Ginsberg took him to meet William Carlos Williams in Paterson, New Jersey. Again Kerouac got drunk, but he behaved himself, and Williams was taken with Corso's work, promising to review his second book. Allen took him to meet surrealist painter Salvador Dalí, who was charmed by Jack's rough-hewn ways.

Kerouac had significantly reworked the text of *On the Road* and spent a good amount of his time in New York City attempting to get libel waivers signed and putting together borrowed sums of money to take a freighter with Corso, Cassady, and Ginsberg to visit Burroughs in Tangier, Morocco.

First, though, Kerouac wanted to see his mother and so climbed aboard a bus to Orlando, where Gabrielle was staying with Carolyn in her new home. Kerouac, drunk on the bus, lost an entire bag of his notes, manuscripts, and revisions and was plunged into despair until a clerk told him that the package had been shipped ahead. After enjoying Christmas with the family, he headed back to New York City and prepared to make a trip to Africa.

Kerouac set sail on the SS *Slovenia* in February, alone. Ginsberg (from whom Kerouac had borrowed the $200 for passage) and Orlovsky were to follow shortly. It was a rough ride for Kerouac, and during a ferocious winter storm, he found himself renouncing his Buddhism and praying once more to the Christian god and studying Kierkegaard's *Fear and Trembling*.

In Africa, he found Burroughs healthy. Kerouac planned originally to spend the rest of the winter and spring in Tangier, and Burroughs was amenable to the idea. In Tangier, Kerouac relaxed in his apartment, which was above Burroughs's place at the Villa Muniria (which he and the other visiting Beats had nicknamed the Villa Delirium), read his books, watched people, and reveled in the good cheap wine and abundant drugs. Good news came in the form of a contract and a £150 check from a British publisher who wanted the U.K. rights to *On the Road*.

After a year in London trying various methods to kick a huge heroin habit, Burroughs was confining himself to opium and hashish in Africa and was putting the finishing touches on a book he called *Word Hoard*, which would be published and become famous under the title *Naked Lunch*. Kerouac availed himself of the prostitutes, and the hash, opium, and amphetamines freely available over the counter in Tangier. The drugs soon took their toll, however, and he became uneasy, having terrible nightmares. Burroughs, though almost free of drugs, had violent mood swings accompanied by personality changes. He took delight in perversity—spitting out his food at an elegant French restaurant, or swinging his machete while describing how he would butcher an Arab boy. Kerouac began to feel a deep depression.

Tangier was cheap enough, and the laws lax enough, that Kerouac could easily have stayed there his planned amount of time, and then some. But soon he grew homesick. The food was bad, he wrote friends; he had dysentery, and he had a drug scare with some hashish that turned out to be laced with arsenic. Burroughs was so deeply in his own mind writing the strange, frightening Beat masterpiece *Naked Lunch* that Kerouac found him impossible to talk to. Jack bided his time, waiting for Ginsberg to make the passage so he would have someone to talk to, but Ginsberg would not arrive until March.

When Ginsberg and Orlovsky arrived, Kerouac's mood lifted for a short time. When he wasn't swimming with them, he would take long hikes by himself into the countryside to sketch the native people. In the end, though, something inside him had changed. He no longer wanted to travel; he wanted to be home. He felt old, especially when confronted with the hipsters barely out of their teens who congregated around Allen, even here in Africa. In late March, Kerouac had two flashes of insight. One was that he simply wasn't now and never could be happy in Morocco, and the second was that he would write his next book about Gary Snyder and their time together in the woods of the Pacific Northwest. Upset and tired, Kerouac tried to sketch out the new book but realized that he would have to go home to the United States to write it.

Kerouac set off again, this times for Paris, via Marseilles, which he reached by ferry from Tangier. In Paris he met up with Gregory Corso, who was now writing pornography for Olympia Press. He and Kerouac took off on the town, but Kerouac had the needling sense that Corso was just humoring him because he had what Corso had none of—money. He played the tourist in both France and London, haunting cathedrals and churches in both places, and in May 1957 returned to America via the elegant ship the *Nieuw Amsterdam*. On the way home, he came up with the somewhat misguided (and most likely drug-addled) idea that to achieve true happiness, he needed to move his mother to Berkeley. Before he left, though, he received an important delivery: a shipment of advance copies of *On the Road*. Cassady was already busy winning free drinks and favors by announcing to anyone who would listen that he was Dean Moriarty.

Chapter 12

FAME

On the Road is a simple story of two young men searching for good times and inner calm. In 1946, Sal Paradise hooks up with Dean Moriarty, a young man from the West, who rekindles the spark of life in the despondent Sal. The plot begins with the narrator, Sal, meeting the manic Dean at a time and place in Sal's life when he feels that everything is falling apart. Dean's presence ignites a wanderlust in Sal and sets him off on a series of cyclic adventures.

Dean Moriarty is a wild man. He steals cars and spends as much time as possible naked. To Dean, people are to be used; they are seen only for what Dean can get out of them. When he's done with them, he abandons them. Yet people continue to be drawn to him. Sal and Dean visit Chicago, where Kerouac introduces one of the defining motifs of *On the Road*—bebop jazz. By the end of the book, Sal realizes that he is searching for the concept of "IT," the understanding of wholeness, of spirituality, of being happy, according to Dean.

The book itself is divided into five parts. The first four detail Sal's adventures on the road—his thoughts and actions during the time he spends traveling, hitchhiking, and riding Greyhound buses, all the while under the shadow of Dean's influence over him—and the fifth draws the cycles to a close.

In part 1, after meeting Dean, Sal sets out to see the frontier, which he, at this point, still identifies with the American Dream. In Denver (which is also Dean's hometown) he meets up with a group of people spanning the artistic spectrum, including Carlo Marx, who had stood as a bridge between Dean and Sal before they actually met in the flesh.

From Denver, Sal heads off to San Francisco, where, meeting up with his old friend Remi Boncourer, he signs on as a security officer but finds himself ill-equipped emotionally for the job. He heads back east on a Greyhound, where he meets a Mexican girl, Terry, with whom he spends a few weeks before returning to the East, where he decides that the frontier, wildness, and freedom that he sought in the West are still available and open to him in the East, that they exist more in his mind than in a locale.

Part 2 begins with Sal and his aunt (with whom he lives) visiting relatives in Virginia. Suddenly Dean appears in a roaring car with his friend Ed Dunkel and Dean's teenage ex-wife Marylou and sweeps Sal off on another wild adventure. In Sal's eyes, Dean has matured from the manic, jittery kid who first asked Sal to teach him to write; Dean has now become something much more in the line of a holy seeker, a pilgrim on a quest. The group drives from Virginia to Paterson, New Jersey, back to Virginia, to New York City to see Carlo Marx, and then down to New Orleans to see Sal's friends, Old Bull Lee and his wife. From there the group runs on to California. In California, Dean does an about-face and deserts Sal and Marylou while he runs off with a new girlfriend, Camille. Sal is crushed and eventually heads back to New York, never caring if he sees Dean again.

Sal is still depressed at the beginning of part 3. He goes back on his decision never to seek out Dean again, tracking him down in hopes of alleviating his slump. Together they make a pact to do everything that they had ever dreamed of but were previously unable to—go to Italy, find Dean's father, with all the excitement of two boys planning a camping trip. Times have changed, however, and now almost everyone who had previously been so drawn to Dean finds him annoying and beat at best, dangerous at worst. Only Sal is willing to stand by him as Dean's friends one by one begin to abandon him. However, by the end of the part, Dean and Sal are fighting. Dean makes an off-the-cuff joke that enrages Sal. In Denver, Sal begins to wonder if the others are right about Dean as he watches Dean's family abandon him. By the time they make it to New York City, the end of their trip, Dean once again abandons Sal for a woman, this time a model named Inez.

Part 4 describes the last attempt at finding the perfect moment on the road. This time Sal and Dean head south of the border to Mexico City and bring with them a new friend, Stan Shepherd. Here Sal believes he will find free and innocent humanity, unfettered by societal rules and constraints. In reality what they find is cheap booze, drugs, and prostitution. When after streaming through the jungle, they finally make it to Mexico

City, Dean again abandons Sal, this time racked with dysentery, to speed back to New York with his Mexican divorce from Camille.

In the novel's final part, Sal's life has reached fruition. He has found the girl for whom he has looked so long and has settled down. This time, when Dean shows up to take him back in search of adventure, Sal refuses. The last image he has of Dean is from the rear seat of the Cadillac in which he is riding on the way to the opera. At the same time, though, Sal realizes that he will always think of Dean when he sees the sun going down in the West.

The theme of *On the Road* begins with a phrase that, many Kerouac critics suggest, sets up a pattern of "collapse and rebirth": "I first met Dean not long after my wife and I split up."[1] The narrative, beginning with an image of collapse, spirals out to rebirth and then collapse and follows these long, circular patterns throughout.

The book is heavy with symbolism. Change in the lives of the characters is marked by the change of the seasons: "New York City, the South and New Orleans in spring; Iowa, Nebraska, Denver, Nevada, St. Louis and Indiana in the fall; and Butte, North Dakota, Portland and Idaho in winter."[2] In addition, there is a complex pattern of color imagery and highly personal symbolism. Finally, there is the element of religious symbolism in the text—the narrator's progression toward "IT," an archetypal quest image.

The character of Sal, the narrator, describes himself as a slightly naive college boy, a serial monogamist, who, while eschewing one-night stands, runs from one deeply felt but short-lived relationship to another. Curiously, Sal admits and knows that he can't trust Dean, that Dean will take advantage of him and leave him, and yet Sal still feels as if he must follow along behind him. Sal is set up as the passive observer (an important change from one of the earlier manuscripts, wherein the two main characters seem to be fighting for dominance, and the question of just whose story the book is remains in doubt). At the end, however, it seems as though Sal is the one who has used Dean. Once Sal has gathered material for the book he is writing and finds his newest girl, Sal leaves Dean alone in the rain.

One of the novel's advance copies made its way into the hands of fill-in *New York Times Book Review* writer Gilbert Millstein, who reviewed it for the September 5, 1957, issue. It was a lucky break—Millstein was young and had already recognized the importance of the Beat writers. The usual reviewer, Orville Prescott, was a hidebound traditionalist, and the book would have suffered a much more brutal fate had it fallen into his hands. Instead, when Kerouac opened the newspaper, he found Millstein's review praising the publication of his work as a "historic occasion...*On the Road* is a major novel." Millstein added that "*On the Road* is the most beautifully executed, the clearest and the most important utterance yet made by the generation Kerouac himself named years ago."[3]

Other publications weren't so kind. Just three days after Millstein's review appeared in the *New York Times*, David Dempsey wrote in the *New York Times Book Review* that "one reads [*On the Road*] in the same mood that he might visit a sideshow—the freaks are fascinating although they are hardly part of our lives." Reviews only got more brutal. The *Herald Tribune* called it "infantile perversely negative," the *Hudson Review* said that reading it was like talking to "a slob running a temperature," and the *Encounter* simply identified it as a "series of Neanderthal grunts."[4] Regardless of the smaller publications' venom, when the *New York Times* talked, people listened, and in the following months, a flood of articles, explaining, expounding on, or simply taking about the Beat generation appeared in *Life*, *Saturday Review*, and many others. *On the Road*, a book Kerouac had written six years before, a book that even he admitted to his friends should be classified in the juvenilia category of his work, which he felt had developed and matured greatly in that time, and a book that presented him as a completely different individual from the one he was now, was on the best-seller list for five weeks, and tens of thousands of people read it and allowed it to change their lives.

Much has been made of the creation of *On the Road*—the legend and mystique that surround the book are not only due to its popularity with readers who are themselves coming of age and searching as the two main characters are. The image of Kerouac, high on speed, sweating through shirt after shirt, guzzling pot after pot of black coffee, all the while typing maniacally at breakneck speed, too busy to revise or self-edit, only spitting out the truth through the clack of the typewriter keys, is an extremely romantic one, and an attractive image of the artist at work for many people. However, even with Kerouac's axiom "First thought best thought," even before the book was published, it had been transformed from the scroll-like teletype (or Japanese drawing paper taped together, depending on the source of the story; Kerouac himself told both versions) to a "450 page manuscript...divided up into its five books, among other changes."[5]

The truth did nothing to deter a thirsty public from buying into the lone-wolf, word-obsessed author sweating off a manuscript and then sending it out to be published. He was immediately famous and immediately in demand. He was offered $100,000 for the movie rights by Warner Brothers (which he didn't take, holding out for a better offer), and profiles of Kerouac appeared in *Esquire* and *Playboy*. Jack enjoyed the money, but not the attention. He sat stock-still in interviews, paralyzed by the fear of saying the wrong thing. Already an alcoholic, he began to consume prodigious amounts of scotch to try to dull the anxiety he felt.

The fame was already preying on his fragile sense of self. Earlier he had written drunkenly to Edie Parker (with whom he hadn't communicated since 1949), saying that Ginsberg's West Coast publicity tour had left him sick to his stomach and wanting to escape reality: "I can't keep up with the hectic fame life [Ginsberg] wants." But that was before Kerouac truly hit it big. When the flood of adulation washed over him, he found it difficult to keep his head above water. John Clellon Holmes said that he felt that Kerouac was "temporarily discombobulated by the image of himself.... He no longer knew who the hell he was supposed to be."[6]

Returning from Tangier and reeling from his sudden thrust into the spotlight, Kerouac struck out on one of the strangest road trips he had ever taken. Desperate for a change and still reminiscing about his time with Snyder on the West Coast, he trundled his mother onto a bus leaving Orlando on May 6, 1957. The two of them got through the trip by washing down aspirin with bourbon and enjoying their stops in New Orleans and El Paso (where they sneaked across the border to Juarez). Then, refreshed by new bottles of booze, they made their way to Los Angeles, then up the coast to Oakland. The trip seemed bizarre even to Jack's closest friends, and to the poets and writers whom he was meeting in Berkeley, it was completely incomprehensible. Kerouac, however, was positive that this was the place to make a fresh start.

Kerouac found his mother and himself a cottage in Berkeley and set some new rules for himself—no more drinking without eating and no giving his address to his old drinking buddies. It was a productive time for him. He revised and expanded his *Book of Dreams*, worked more on *Old Angel Midnight*, wrote up his trip to Tangier in a collection called "A Dharma Bum in Europe," and even started a new novel, which he was calling "Avalokitesvara." He drew portraits of his friend Philip Whalen, and pietas as well. During this time, though, Kerouac's commitment to Buddhism continued to wane as he tried to find a way to combine Buddhism and Catholicism into one religion. His mother continued to ride him about everything, infantilizing him and complaining about the weather, the climate, the mountains, and how much she missed Florida. Finally Jack agreed to head back to Florida, and the two bought tickets to return there in mid-July 1957.

Kerouac was miserable in Florida, as well. He was staying with his sister and brother-in-law again, who had already expressed their dislike for his lifestyle. Added to the problem was the fact that his room had no air-conditioning, which meant that he had to keep the door open, and leaving the door to his room open meant that the rest of the family had complete access to him and also that they could, legitimately, claim that his typing was bothering them. Finally, the pressure was too much. He packed his rucksack again and headed to Mexico City on July 23, 1957.

He didn't last there. Everything, Kerouac found, had changed. Bill Garver, a friend Kerouac had met through Burroughs, had died of an overdose. Esperanza, his model for *Tristessa*, had disappeared. Kerouac checked into a fancy hotel, locked himself into his room, and sat around smoking marijuana. The 1957 earthquake hit Mexico City, causing death and damage. Psychically, it was too much for him. He felt that he couldn't write any longer. He packed his bag and headed back to Florida and his mother.

In Florida, Malcolm Cowley wrote to Jack asking for a childhood book of Lowell free of the conceit of *Doctor Sax*. But Kerouac's once-vaunted memory had been ravaged by decades of alcohol abuse. He simply couldn't remember enough of such a long time ago to put a book together. Instead he fueled himself on amphetamines and sat down at his typewriter to complete the story of his meeting Gary Snyder and his time in the fire tower. He called it *The Dharma Bums* and finished it by December 9.

In February 1958 Kerouac was once again drinking heavily, but he was still able to hide the toll that alcohol was taking on his body from his friends. On weeklong drinking binges, he could still outdrink everyone and still had the tremendous physical strength that had made him such an athlete in his youth. Gregory Corso, for example, according to Nicosia, couldn't understand why Jack was so miserable. He was, after all, famous and (at least compared to Corso) rich. Kerouac fought endlessly with his mother but nonetheless convinced her to move from Florida back to New York. Kerouac headed off to Long Island to find a new home. But the entire time, he was headed toward a crack-up. He told Ginsberg that he felt rejected by the culture, saying that America was caught up in a "Fall." Corso again told Kerouac that he was confused by his behavior, saying that "the person who creates a new society will have no place in that society himself."[7] Kerouac found this to be cold comfort.

Meanwhile, on the West Coast, Cassady was getting more and more out of control. Always outrageous and a magnet for cops, he began acting more and more erratically, taunting the undercover cops and waving to the policemen who had been sent to watch him. Carolyn wrote that she felt something had changed inside Neal, that he was harder, angrier, and cockier. Finally Cassady crossed the line one too many times and was arrested on what appeared to be trumped-up charges.

Jack was furious at Cassady. It was almost as if Kerouac felt that Cassady had let him down by not escaping the long arm of the law again, like a cartoon character who always just gets away before being captured. Kerouac cut him off, seemingly unaware that his glorification and promotion of Neal had anything at all to do with Cassady's rise to notoriety.

In March 1958, Kerouac found a home in Northport, Long Island, to move his mother and cats and himself to. It was old and large with front and back porches and, although just 50 miles from New York City, was quiet and had a distinct New England feel. There were pine trees in the yard under which to meditate. Again Jack felt that maybe this was a place where he could settle down and live a quieter life. His mother set down rules: no drugs in the house, not even Kerouac's Benzedrine, and no unsuitable characters, either. This excluded almost all Jack's friends, in her eyes. She even wrote Ginsberg, threatening to turn him in to the FBI if he showed up at the door. As always, Jack blustered, then acquiesced.

Kerouac killed the weeks until he could move in by sleeping in friends' Manhattan apartments. It was not his best hour. Outside a bar, he was beaten horribly and ended up bleeding from the head so heavily that he had to be taken to the hospital. Years later Kerouac would say that he thought he had received some sort of brain injury that night, but by the time he told his friends, it was much too late to do anything about it. He gave a bizarre lecture at Brooklyn College, where he was mobbed by 2,000 students, who were mostly confused when he answered their questions with what he thought to be Zen koans. On a publicity tour, when he appeared on *Nightbeat* and was asked by the host, "What is a mainliner?" Kerouac answered by singing "Skyliner." Finally, overcoming his natural shyness with gallons of liquor, he performed for a week as master of ceremonies for poetry readings at the Circle in the Square Theater.

His bizarre behavior, perhaps designed to test people or make them reveal their true selves, did nothing to help the problems that Kerouac found himself in. Far from turning people off, or reeducating them, it only reinforced his image as a "kooky beatnik." Increasingly his manic, nonsensical act was shoving people away. When he stopped at *Esquire* magazine to discuss an idea for an article he had, he thought that the editor was asking too many questions and not trusting Jack enough as a great writer. To get his opinion across, he took off his shirt while the editor was talking, folded it, put it on the floor, and, using it as a pillow, went to sleep. The article, it is perhaps needless to say, was not sold.

Back in Northport, Kerouac told people that he was still working on *Memory Babe*, which he now said would be an intensive, Joycean study of 1935 Christmas weekend in Lowell. In truth, much of the time when he said he was working, he was actually wandering in the backyard and singing to himself. He fought with the publisher of *The Dharma Bums*, Viking Press, who had inserted commas into his long sentences to make the text more manageable. Kerouac felt it was butchery, and when he insisted that the original sentence structure be restored, Viking did so and then charged him $500 that he didn't have for the printer's fees. Kerouac was incensed, and that charge (which he refused to pay), as well as Viking's refusal to publish *Visions of Gerard*, led to his separation with the publisher. He was still flogging other projects as well. Late in the spring, MGM bought the movie rights to *The Subterraneans* for $15,000, and a small company, Tri-Way Productions, purchased the rights to *On the Road* for $25,000, of which Kerouac only saw $2,500 before the company collapsed under bankruptcy.

In early spring of 1958, Kerouac made a recording that would introduce him to a much wider audience. The record, for Dot Records, featured Steve Allen on piano while Kerouac read from various journals and unpublished works. Recorded in one take, the album showed an author who was using his voice as an instrument. It was a beautiful piece of work, coming on the heels of one of Kerouac's slower times. The administration at Dot Records, however, decided that some of the selections Jack read were in bad taste and waited for a year before distributing it, titled *Poetry for the Beat Generation*. Two other recordings, *Readings on the Beat Generation* and *Blues and Haikus*, are notable mostly for the backing jazz artists, who included Zoot Sims and Al Cohn.

The stress of fame was leading Kerouac to feel his age. His mother worried about him and worked to isolate him from his friends whom she deemed dangerous. She continued to read the letters that Ginsberg sent him and then wrote him back, warning him to stay away from her and her home. Jack would later say to Allen that he agreed with her that he was too old for the life he was living and just wanted to disappear into a world of childish daydreams. Neal's arrest had made him paranoid about associating with drug users, and his fear of jail was so strong that he refused to go to the West Coast to go hiking with his friends. Even his old stomping grounds were becoming off-limits. When he found graffiti in the restroom of a Manhattan tavern, the White Horse, that read "Kerouac go home," he did just that and avoided the bar, fearing that people were out to get him.

By April 1958, the fame and his drinking showed no signs of slowing down. Whether Kerouac was an idiot or a savant was a hotly waged battle among the critics. In the meantime, Grove Press published *The Subterraneans* to ride on the coattails of the *On the Road* success. The critics savaged it. The *New Republic* wrote that "nowhere is there any sign that either the author or his characters know what they are talking about." According to Nicosia, "*The New York Times*...quipped that the story 'seeps out here, like sludge from a leaky drain pipe.' " *Time* announced that Kerouac "is not Rimbaud but a kind of latrine laureate of Hobohemia," as well as a "cut rate Thomas Wolfe." *Time* magazine made no attempt to hide its aversion to Kerouac's characters, calling them "ambisextruous and hipsterical" and linking their "madness" to drug use. *Newsweek* called the novel "a tasteless account of a love affair between a white man and a Negro girl."[8]

Kerouac was crushed, especially when Rexroth threw his two cents in as well. Following his review of *The Subterraneans*, which contained the line, "This book is about jazz and Negroes, two things Jack knows nothing about," Rexroth started his review of *The Dharma Bums* with a line that would become famous: "Someone once said of Mr. Kerouac that he was a Columbia freshman who went to a party in the village twenty years ago and got lost. How true. The naïve effrontery of this book is more pitiful than ridiculous."[9] It hurt Jack deeply, especially since he had been sending apologies and notes of reconciliation to Rexroth for some time.

Viking had purchased his manuscript of *The Dharma Bums*, which dealt with the time he had spent with Gary Snyder and on Desolation Mountain. *The Dharma Bums* had been conceived originally as a sequel to *On the Road*, and the two make an interesting pair to read side by side. The plot of *The Dharma Bums* takes place six years after the events relayed in *On the Road*. The main characters, based on Kerouac, Cassady, and Ginsberg, reappear (under different names) in the text and are joined by the new hero, Japhy Ryder (based on the Californian poet Gary Snyder). Also telling as to how the two books are related, the Kerouac character's name is Ray Smith (the narrator), a name that Kerouac had originally used as the narrator's name in an early draft of *On the Road*.

Kerouac tells the story in 34 chapters, although the text does lend itself to being split into three parts. In the first part, Ray Smith meets Japhy Ryder, and their friendship develops in episodes detailed in San Francisco, Berkeley, and the High Sierras. The first section begins with a description of one of the most famous poetry readings of the twentieth century—the Six Gallery reading at which Allen Ginsberg first read *Howl* and all the major members of what would come to be known as the San Francisco Poetry Renaissance performed. Interestingly, Kerouac downplays the reading of *Howl* (which he calls "Wail") and focuses on the reading of quiet, self-assured woodsman-poet Gary Snyder, whom he calls Japhy Ryder. In fact, the entire reading is downplayed in favor of a long description of Kerouac's climbing of the California Matterhorn. Smith then takes off, hitchhiking across the country to spend the winter in North Carolina with his mother and sister and her family. Before long, though, Smith's new Buddhist ways start to conflict with his mother's vision of what he should be doing. In response, Smith gets back on the road, back to the West Coast, where he meets up with Ryder and shares a cabin with him before Ryder sets off on a ship for a stay at a Zen monastery. Japhy impresses Ray with his simple lifestyle and the easy, nonchalant way in which he attracts women, even though he is committed to chastity outside of his relationship with his girlfriend. On their second trip to the mountains (joined this time by new friend Henry Moore), the two climb joyously, shouting haikus and Zen koans (riddles without answers designed to shock the mind into emptiness).

In the middle third of the novel, Kerouac introduces the concept that most readers remember from the book—the "rucksack revolution"—Kerouac's idea that by embracing the simple ideas of Japhy, millions of American youths will feel free to hit the roads with their backpacks and abandon the consumer culture that was just starting to take over America. Ray comes back to California and finds himself unable or unwilling to adapt to civilization. He heads to North Carolina to spend Christmas with his mother and sister's family and stays there until spring, meditating in the woods, where he begins to see visions of himself as Buddha. This experience refuels Ray's desire to see Japhy again, and he begins to make plans to head to California.

The novel's third part finds Ray in what he terms as heaven—he's back in California and has found free shelter, staying with a Buddhist family in wooded, beautiful Marin County. He soon tires, though, of the endless drunken parties and wants to head back to the woods. Japhy feels sick of culture too, however, and heads to Japan to study in a Buddhist monastery that has agreed to accept him. Smith takes Ryder's advice and heads off to the Washington State woods to find himself by isolating himself completely by working as a fire ranger in a mountaintop tower. The last advice Japhy gives him, Ray accepts—he applies and is chosen for a job as a fire lookout on Desolation Peak, a mountaintop in Washington's Cascade Mountains, where he feels that he receives another vision before he heads back to the wild life whose call he hears and follows back to civilization. The book seems to end abruptly. Although as readers we are led to believe that the climax of the book will take place at the fire lookout, it never occurs. In actuality, Kerouac had a difficult time in the fire tower. He was overwhelmed by the isolation, had a hard time drying out from his alcohol abuse, and was tortured with guilt after killing a mouse. Like Smith,

Kerouac was relieved to go back to Seattle, pick up some cheap wine, and check into a skid row hotel to get drunk.

Ray Smith is a man torn between the two lives he wishes to lead. On the one hand, he wishes to live a quiet, contemplative life, but on the other, anytime the opportunity to get drunk and wild presents itself, he takes it. He wants to travel, but when he is gone, he longs to be home with his mother.

In Japhy Ryder, by contrast, Kerouac has created a whole character—Japhy is at home wherever he is and is always self-sufficient. He is, of course, most happy in the woods, where he has a comfort level that makes Ray envious.

Perhaps most important, *The Dharma Bums* functions as a simple record of life in artistic America in the 1950s—the reader is treated to what it was like to be with the Bay Area writers and artists in 1955. This strength, though, is oftentimes the book's downfall—too many of Kerouac's sketches are never fully fleshed out.

The book was finished in ten-speed, coffee-fueled typing sessions and passed effortlessly into the editorial stream at Viking, since the manuscript was bereft of Kerouac's experimental text and didn't require extensive editorial wrangling. Under the advice of editor Malcolm Cowley, Kerouac had written a popular book for a quick paycheck. Without his stress on experimental text, *The Dharma Bums* represents the sort of book that he could have churned out endlessly, providing him with a comfortable means of support had he not turned his efforts strictly to what he would have termed art over commercialism. At the same time, however, the popularity of *On the Road* and *The Dharma Bums*, with their relatively clear language and plots, set Kerouac up for disaster when the work that followed, with its much more complicated plots, language, and style, failed to fulfill the reading public's expectations.

The reviews of *The Dharma Bums* were no better than those of his previous novels. This one suffered because the book seemed calculated to achieve a popular reading audience, so that those who had begun to accept Kerouac as an experimental artist were disappointed that he had written such a traditionally formatted book. Seymour Krim wrote in his article "King of the Beats" in *Commonweal* magazine on January 2, 1959, that "Ray Smith, the hero of the present chapter in Kerouac's nonstop gush...adds mountain climbing and meditating to the typical Kerouacian staple of batting madly around the country....Literary teetotalers and nice little old ladies...forget that he loves (but loves, man!) his booze and sex as much as ever; his next book may very well revive the original horror and condemnation."[10]

NOTES

1. Jack Kerouac, *On the Road* (New York: Viking, 1976), p. 3.

2. Gerald Nicosia, *Memory Babe* (Berkeley: University of California Press, 1994), p. 271.

3. Gilbert Millstein, review of *On the Road*, by Jack Kerouac, *New York Times*, 5 September 1957.

4. Nicosia, *Memory Babe*, p. 556.

5. Nicosia, *Memory Babe*, p. 556.

6. Nicosia, *Memory Babe*, p. 576.

7. Nicosia, *Memory Babe*, p. 576.

8. Nicosia, *Memory Babe*, p. 568.

9. Ann Charters, *Kerouac* (San Francisco: Straight Arrow Books, 1973), p. 308.

10. Seymour Krim, "King of the Beats," *Commonweal*, 2 January 1959, p. 32.

Chapter 13

THE BEATNIK BACKLASH

Kerouac, looking for some peace and quiet away from the maelstrom of fame that had engulfed him, had purchased a home on the North Shore of Long Island and moved his mother and their cats to the town of Northport. Even here, though, people soon got wind of where and who he was. Fans zoomed up in the middle of the night to go drinking or on wild adventures, and Kerouac found it difficult to say no to any of them. Meanwhile Kenneth Rexroth nursed an angry, resentful jealousy of Kerouac in the papers and small magazines of the times. Neal Cassady was thrown in jail on marijuana charges. All these things contributed to Kerouac's general anxiety and his sense that he was somehow responsible for all the problems; they had, after all, arisen at the same time as his good fortune.

That bad luck would soon extend itself to Jack. In a pattern familiar to all students of the American media, the press that had once hailed the newness and excitement of the Beat generation soon grew tired of it and moved to more "interesting" topics. The Beat writers, once lionized, were now demonized in the press, both academic and popular. Magazines and journals as varied as the *Partisan Review* and *Playboy* bemoaned the desecration of propriety, the rampant drug use, the contribution to the moral decay of society that they expected (though only sometimes found) within the Beat culture. Ironically, Kerouac's politics were far right of center, and he was, as was the mainstream political flavor of the time, a strident anticommunist. He said little, though, to defend himself, suffering in silence; and matters certainly weren't helped by Ginsberg's and Corso's published defenses of the movement. Corso's "Variations on a Generation," appearing in the *Village Voice* in 1959, featured lines like "The Beat

Generation is high, is good omen, is like frog." In the midst of all this anti-Beat attitude, *The Dharma Bums* was savaged by the critical and academic press. Critics who were unaware of the time lapse between *On the Road*, *The Subterraneans*, and *The Dharma Bums* believed that the books had been written in tandem with, rather than separate from, the Kerouac media circus.

On January 2, 1959, Kerouac, Ginsberg, and others got together to make a movie, *Pull My Daisy* (originally Kerouac wanted to call it *The Beat Generation*, only to discover that the title had long been copyrighted by MGM). The budget was $15,000, mainly supported by the Dreyfus Fund. The idea had percolated from a Kerouac friend and photographer, Robert Frank. He was in the process of making what he saw as a trilogy of films. Originally Frank and his partner Al Leslie had wanted to film *On the Road* but felt that driving, scouting, and filming all the widespread locales would be too difficult and expensive. Instead Jack let them listen to a tape recording he called "The Beat Generation," which was snatches of conversation and jazz recorded from the radio. After listening to it, they decided to make a silent film of act 3, which told the story of a bishop coming to visit the Cassadys. Then, after the film was finished, Kerouac would read all the dialogue for the actors, who would be filmed moving their lips.

The play/movie retells the story of Neal and Carolyn, Allen and Peter, and Jack going to see a progressive bishop speak in California in 1955. The Cassadys invited the bishop back to the house; he agreed and brought with him his mother and aunt. Allen plunked himself down on the couch between the two ladies and started asking the bishop about sex. Jack, drunk, sat on the floor alternately clutching a gallon jug of wine and the bishop's leg, murmuring, "I love you!"

They planned to shoot a minute of action each day. Leslie read the lines out loud, and then the actors mouthed the words back. Before long, Leslie gave up any attempt at directing them and just let them improvise. Kerouac and Leslie didn't get along. Leslie was an African American Jew and felt that Kerouac's reverence for African Americans was a sort of reverse discrimination and that his anti-Semitism was appalling. Kerouac in turn took every chance to ridicule Leslie's penchant for intellectual discussion The last straw came when Kerouac dragged a filthy bum covered with oozing boils up to the set to have a drink. When Leslie attacked Kerouac for his unprofessionalism, he began singing. Leslie banished him from the set.

The filming took six weeks, and by the time Leslie had finished the final cut, the film ran 90 minutes long. Kerouac's contribution provided new problems. When, in Northport, they sat down to do the voices to match the mouth movements of the characters, it became clear that Kerouac was incapable of doing the job. Leslie went back and cut the film to 29 minutes and then allowed Kerouac to simply riff over it. Again Kerouac exasperated Leslie. He did the narration once in a stereotypical Chinese accent, then a narration all in French, describing the events as if they were taking place in Lowell. Kerouac left the studio believing that he had done a good job. Leslie wasn't convinced.

Instead of using one of the narrations intact, Leslie spliced all of them together, including the original tape recording that Kerouac had let him listen to in the first place. Today *Pull My Daisy* is seen as one of the first underground films, as well as a major influence on the films of artists like Andy Warhol. The experimental film is more than anything a montage of Ginsberg, Corso, and Orlovsky, nude much of the time, with a narrative thread wound very loosely by Kerouac's voice-over. It received, as one might assume, poor reviews, with the interesting exception of well-respected critic and director Peter Bogdanovich, who praised it endlessly. Kerouac was furious with Leslie's splicings, but his opinion soon mellowed when the film began to be hailed as an inaugural piece of the American New Wave (echoing a term that had recently been applied to experimental French films).

His popularity continued to isolate Kerouac from everyone and drive him more deeply into the bottle. By the beginning of 1959, Kerouac was spending more and more time alone in Northport, drunk. His promising relationship with Dody Muller, widow of the painter Jan Muller, which had the potential of helping to normalize some small part of Kerouac's life, was quickly ended by his mother. In fact, Kerouac had even debated asking Muller to marry him and move to Paris, a plan quickly shot down by his obsessive worries about what would happen to his mother—as well as his mother's actions. Dody was required to wear a hair net in the kitchen, and if she washed the dishes, Kerouac's mother would quickly empty the clean dishes back into the sink and rewash them. Kerouac's mother called Dody "the Savage" and at one point accused her of being a witch and using voodoo rituals to steal Kerouac away from her. Kerouac went along with all of it, placating his mother. Muller, in fact, made the comment with which so many others would soon agree: Kerouac's already Oedipal relationship with his mother had progressed to the point where the distinction between son and husband (with the exception of sexual relations) no longer existed. When Kerouac's mother once again banned Ginsberg from their house because of her rabid anti-Semitism, Kerouac acquiesced.

He buried any regrets he might have had in his work. By the spring of 1959, he began to write a column for the magazine *Escapade*, began editing a thrice-yearly Beat writers anthology for Avon Books, and prepared the galleys for his books that would appear on the shelves in the next year and a half: *Maggie Cassidy, Tristessa, Mexico City Blues, The Scripture of the Golden Eternity, Visions of Cody,* and *Pull My Daisy.* This hectic schedule was slapdash work on the part of publishers. Work was being sent out with little or no thought to order or quality, simply to fulfill market demand. While Kerouac corrected his prepublication work, he drank whiskey, and before long, he was consuming a quart of bourbon a day.

Throwing himself into his work, he began final drafts of what would become *Maggie Cassidy,* a book that dwells on Kerouac's experiences of first love that he found in Lowell with a 17-year-old working-class girl. The story is told through three separate perspectives as time passes. The story is told through the eyes of Jack at 16, 20, and 32 years old, covering the years from 1939, when he was a Lowell High School football star, to the year 1943, when he first shipped out as a merchant mariner.

The book idealizes woman as all the others do. In the first chapters we find Maggie to be the perfect woman for Jack to play out all his adolescent fantasies. He dreams of being her "brother, husband, lover, raper, owner, friend, father, son, grabber, kisser, keener, swain, sneaker-upper, sleeper-with, feeler, railroadbrakeman in red house..."[1] The last phrase refers to Maggie's request (as Jack's real first girlfriend also requested) that the writer stay in Lowell and marry her and work on the railroad. Jack refuses to do so, associating marriage (perhaps rightly so) with the end of boyhood freedom.

Kerouac was having a burst of creative energy, the kind that was occurring more and more rarely. To capitalize on it and to get away from the teenagers who flocked to his Northport home, he decided the best course of action was to head back to Mexico City and complete *Desolation Angels.* He planned on calling the second half "Beat Traveler" and using it to chronicle the time between the moment he left Mexico City in 1956 and the moment of his rise to fame in New York with the publication of *On the Road.*

First, though, as always, he had to take care of his mother. Separated from her daughter, Gabrielle was feeling more and more lonely. Kerouac and she put together the plan of building a duplex in Florida for them all to live in. Jack planned on making sure that they bought wooded lots around the duplex to afford them privacy. Kerouac was so excited about the project that he offered to pay for most of it. As Nicosia relates, "He wrote Nin that the house in Northport, which he owned clear, was worth

$14,000 and he had $3,000 in the bank, $8,000 in royalties coming in April and the final installment of $12,000 from MGM for *The Subterraneans* due in June. Nor would he require Paul [his brother-in-law] to pay him back, although he suggested that when Paul could afford it he might contribute to Memere's living expenses."[2]

The spring of 1959 brought bad news as well, though. Gary Snyder had cut Kerouac off when *The Dharma Bums* was published. Jack was destroyed and wrote Snyder pleading letters, trying to explain that he had written the book in a sincere and honest appreciation of all the branches of Buddhism. Gary wrote him back "only to describe a certain hell where writers have their tongues pulled out."[3] Snyder was so upset because he now was suffering through what Kerouac had already experienced—now when people met Snyder, they wanted him to do a Japhy Ryder act, and when he didn't live up to the book's character, people told him how disappointing it was to find him. Snyder was unwilling to put on drunken-clown acts like Kerouac was. It was only after Snyder left for Japan to go back to a Zen monastery and away from people who had ever heard of *The Dharma Bums* that he was ready and willing to resume his friendship with Kerouac.

On April 30, 1959, Kerouac had another blow to his ego. On that day, Grove Press released *Dr. Sax*. Kerouac knew what was coming and couldn't face the reviews firsthand. He asked a friend to read them to him over his phone. Nicosia writes that "Barnaby Conrad in *The Saturday Review* [wrote]: 'I can hardly bring myself to call it a novel.'...Conrad contented himself with listing everything Kerouac's writing lacked—'charm and compassion and invention'—and filled out the review with several complaints about Kerouac's 'dirty words.' This level of criticism was fully matched by David Dempsey in the *New York Times*, who railed against the fact that such an 'unreadable' and 'psychopathic' book had even been published, and by *The Atlantic* calling it 'juvenile scrimshaw'; and by the *New York Herald Tribune* calling it 'boring.' "[4]

In June 1959, Kerouac had made the final arrangements and was ready to move back to Florida with his mother to be with his sister. Kinks had surfaced in his plan. Paul, Nin's husband, still nursing a deep dislike of Jack, had nixed the idea of a family communal duplex and had instead insisted on building two separate houses, but using the same idea of multiple lots strung together. Jack's mother went ahead to Florida to set up housekeeping while Kerouac stayed in Northport (the buyers of his home wouldn't be moving in until August) and then decided to move off for a writing vacation in Mexico City.

In August 1959, however, his mother wrote to tell him that family tensions were running too high for her to feel comfortable living in Florida any longer. Kerouac's sister and brother-in-law were having problems with their marriage. She was sure that he has having an affair, and the family had decided that having Kerouac and his mother living there as well would only make matters worse. Kerouac hustled to make sure that he had a house with an area big enough for him to work by the time she made it back.

By mid-November 1959, both he and his mother were drinking to afternoon unconsciousness regularly. Kerouac had begun to experience the delirium tremens. He had fought viciously with Ginsberg again, and Ginsberg himself had begun to feel like he was being pulled into the madness that surrounded the popularity of the Beats, which he had avoided for so long.

Kerouac had been avoiding any public appearances, but when invited to appear on *The Steve Allen Show*, he accepted because it was one of his mother's favorite shows. More pragmatically, he had been offered $2,000 to do the show, and of course it would be free publicity on a show that regularly drew 30 million viewers. Because all he had were ragged "beat" clothes, he went to purchase some "fancy" clothes for his TV appearance. He bought a pair of gray slacks and a gray tweed jacket. The next time he wore the jacket would be in his casket.

Kerouac was drunk when he appeared on *The Steve Allen Show* that month, and in San Francisco, attending the International Film Festival, where *Pull My Daisy* had been entered, he stalked around in a plaid shirt, drunk and angry, and at one point fell off the stage during a lecture. At a poetry reading at the Living Theatre, Kerouac, who was not scheduled to read, propped himself up onstage and drunkenly heckled the readers. The painters Franz Kline and Willem de Kooning tried to physically restrain him; finally when Kerouac told Frank O'Hara that his reading was "all yatter and no poetry" and suddenly stood up shouting, "You're ruining American poetry, O'Hara," the writer, who had been respectful so far, shut Kerouac up with a withering, "That's more than you could ever do."[5]

Kerouac's cracks, caused by fame, were showing ever and ever more clearly. Scheduled to visit Neal in prison, Jack collapsed drunkenly and refused to go, finally convincing fellow alcoholic poet Lew Welch to drive him cross-country back to Northport to check on his mother. He came home to the new furor that had arisen over the release of the movie *The Subterraneans*, based on his novel of the same name.

The Subterraneans movie was as mainstream, middle-American as Beat culture was outsider culture. Instead of glorifying or providing a window on the beliefs and lives of the Beats as Kerouac had intended, the movie relied on clichés and stereotypes already developed by the American media. The Hollywood version toned down what had been an incredibly controversial part of the book—the interracial love affair between the narrator and Mardou. When the book was published, the critics suggested that it would, in the words of a *Partisan Review* critic, promote "primitivism." The silver screen sought to sidestep such volatile pre-civil-rights-era questions by ignoring them and providing clichés rather than characters. Patrick Mullins, in "Hollywood and the Beats," believes that these one-dimensional portrayals may have been due to a number of factors.[6] It may have been that the screenwriters had little or no experience or meetings with the Beat authors and thus truly believed that their portrayals were accurate. It may have been that the writers knew that their audience would expect to see bongos and goatees and sought to fulfill their expectations, or it may have been a conscious attempt to neutralize the revolutionary power of the Beat movement by making them seem clownish. No matter what the intention, however, Kerouac and the rest of the Beats were disgusted by the movie.

In October 1959, Kerouac suffered another blow when *Mexico City Blues* was released. As usual, the reviews were brutal, but the one that hurt him the most was the one written for the *New York Times* by Kenneth Rexroth. Rexroth was as vengeful as he had been in the past, calling the book nothing but Buddhist idolatry. Kerouac was so upset that he wrote Snyder asking him how Rexroth could be so vehemently anti-Kerouac when he had once been one the greatest supporters of the Beats. Snyder had not succor for him.

NOTES

1. Jack Kerouac, *Maggie Cassidy* (New York: Avon Books, 1959), p. 77.

2. Gerald Nicosia, *Memory Babe* (Berkeley: University of California Press, 1994), p. 586.

3. Nicosia, *Memory Babe*, p. 587.

4. Nicosia, *Memory Babe*, p. 587.

5. Nicosia, *Memory Babe*, p. 592.

6. Patrick Mullins, "Hollywood and the Beats: MGM does Kerouac's *The Subterraneans*," *Journal of Popular Film and Television* (Spring 2001), p. 34.

Chapter 14

DECLINE

The world in 1960 had grown tired of the Beats. Jonathan Paul Eburne, in his essay "Trafficking in the Void," writes: "Divulging his latest platform as crime and commie busting, director of the FBI J. Edgar Hoover claimed at the 1960 Republican Convention that 'beatniks' were, alongside communists and liberal 'eggheads,' one of the three greatest risks to U.S. National Security."[1]

At the beginning of 1960, back in Northport, Kerouac continued drinking. Although he claimed it was to ease the stress of bad reviews and the betrayal he felt at the Hollywoodization of *The Subterraneans*, which had just reached theaters offering up George Peppard as the Kerouac character, it was clear to those surrounding Jack that he was in the latter stages of alcoholism.

Kerouac had stopped eating almost entirely and only drank. He was feeling trapped in Northport by his fame, and when he wasn't drunk, he was arguing with his mother. In April 1960 he fell down drunk in Penn Station and badly injured his elbow. In May, during a weeklong binge in the Bowery, he fell and hit his head so hard that his friends thought he was going to die.

And yet the spring of 1960 should have been a triumphant one. Nicosia writes, "The New Directions limited edition of *Visions of Cody* was selling out. LeRoi Jones published his long poem 'Rimbaud' in *Yugen* and brought out *The Scriptures of the Golden Eternity* with his Totem Press. Avon issued *Tristessa* in June. McGraw-Hill had accepted a collection of his *Holiday* pieces called *Lonesome Traveler*, to be published in the fall. Ferlinghetti had agreed to do a selection from the *Book of Dreams* with

City Lights. Jack's books were being translated in twenty languages, including Japanese. There was a new Hanover record of him reading blues and haikus with jazz responses from Al Cohn and Zoot Sims, and the movie of *The Subterraneans* would be released in July. Though Avon, under new ownership, had canceled his Beat Anthology, he was (and would be) featured prominently in a variety of current and coming anthologies, among the most notable *The Beat Generation and the Angry Young Men*, Seymour Krim's *The Beats*, Don Allen's *The New American Poetry 1945–1960*, *The Beat Scene*, Thomas Parkinson's *A Casebook on the Beat*, and LeRoi Jones's *The Moderns*."[2]

Kerouac had taken down his dreams for decades before compiling them for Lawrence Ferlinghetti. (Although on July 11, 1967, he wrote an admirer that he had given up on it: "No longer write down my dreams on waking, too lazy for now, but used to, between 1952 and 1960, all in *Book of Dreams*. But do make definite habit of mulling them over in detail on waking nowadays, and am keeping track of strange reoccurrences and even have a dream novel in mind.... I like to sleep so I can tune in see what's happening in the big show....I'd rather dream than sit around bleakly with bores in 'real' life.")[3]

The *Book of Dreams* had been kicking around in Kerouac's head for quite some time. He mentioned it to his agent, Sterling Lord, in a letter dated January 23, 1955. Apparently, however, the manuscript wasn't in any sort of form that Lord could read. Two years later, on February 4, 1957, Kerouac was still working on the project. In a letter to his editor at Viking Press, Malcolm Cowley, Kerouac wrote that he had it in his possession and chided Cowley for not including it in the list of books that Kerouac had available for sale or publication: "BOOK OF DREAMS...a 300-page tome of some excellence, spontaneously written dreams some of them written in the peculiar dream-language of half-awake in the morning."[4]

In the book, Kerouac seems to feel that he is refining his spontaneous prose as well as working on finding a fresh way to describe things and make sense of the world around him. The book also shows his overall disgust at the concepts of traditional literature, such as unity of plot. What was more important, he wrote, was capturing the dreams as they come.

The book exists in two versions. One is the 1961 version that Ferlinghetti published through City Lights. For it, Kerouac typed up a collection of dreams that he had been recording in his notebooks for decades. Then Ferlinghetti selected from those poems the ones he wished to publish. Those selections went back to Kerouac, who made small changes such as correcting typographical errors and of course changing characters' names to "protect" his friends (in reality to protect Ferlinghetti from libel or slander suits).

In the edition published in 2001 with a foreword by Kerouac's friend and fellow poet Robert Creeley, the editors included the full collection of Kerouac's manuscript (provided, by the way, by Sterling Lord) while attempting to make corrections that Kerouac may have made himself (perhaps easier said than done) and preserving many of the most obvious typographical errors on the theory that Kerouac himself had plenty of chances to correct them before sending the manuscript to Lord and that these typographical errors might be mental slips that reveal more of Kerouac's psyche—the entire theory after all, of collecting one's dreams.

Kerouac himself says in the introduction that this book was the easiest one to write. His process went like this, he said: on awakening, he would give himself a minute to remember and ponder what he had dreamed and then furiously scribble it all down without any editing, claiming that "being half awake I hardly knew what I was doing let alone writing."[5] Most interesting, he says that sometimes after fully waking, he would be embarrassed or ashamed of what he had written, but he revisited the urge, he claimed, to revise what the dream had contained. He finished, in true Kerouac style, by prescribing his method for everyone. When he found something good, he wanted to share it with everyone.

In Northport, he continued drinking, unable to stop now. He felt that being removed from everyone might clear his mind enough, might help him to at least slow down his rate of intoxication. He went to Pennsylvania's Pocono Mountains in search of a cabin in the wilderness. Instead he was mugged and stranded there. His work had slowed again, and he was unable to bring his thoughts together to form any sort of comprehensible narrative. He fought more and more with Ginsberg and defended his mother with new ferocity. In May 1960 he began to experience the delirium tremens.

When Ferlinghetti heard of his troubles, he invited Kerouac to use his cabin in Big Sur, California, as an escape, a place to be alone. When Kerouac left Long Island in July 1960, he planned on drying out on the train trip to California and staying at the cabin until October. It was as if he had learned nothing from his sojourn in the Pacific Northwest, where the solitude as a fire watcher had crippled him psychically and emotionally.

After hiding himself away for three days in the sleeping compartment with the instant coffee and sandwiches that his mother had made and packed for him, he arrived in California, pushing 40 years of age, lonely, sad, and drunk, and immediately began a three-day bender, missing his ride with Ferlinghetti to the cabin. Making his way via bus and cab, Kerouac arrived in Big Sur late in the evening and stumbled through the woods, unable to find the cabin. He began to panic and threw down his sleeping bag where he was to sleep the night away. In the morning, he found the cabin and settled in for three weeks, chopping wood and reading *Dr. Jekyll and Mr. Hyde* by lantern light.

Kerouac was uneasy from the beginning of his stay, however. He saw one of the local mountains and identified it with a disturbing drug-induced vision he had experienced in Mexico City years earlier. In the vision, winged horses circled the mountain, and Kerouac believed that something incredibly sinister had to be going on there because any of the Mexicans he asked about what he was watching refused to talk to him about it.

Pushing his fear back down, Kerouac sat down to work on a long stream-of-consciousness poem in the style of *Old Angel Midnight* that he was calling "Sea." In it he attempted to capture the actual voice of the ocean, the sounds that it made as it crashed and sallied against the shore near the cabin. All the focus on the sea, though, and the image of the "evil" mountain looming over him were too much for him. Three weeks after arriving, Kerouac had an anxiety attack and a hallucination in which he believed that the sea was yelling at him to leave. He took the hallucination's advice and hitchhiked back to San Francisco, where he immediately took up drinking at the same extreme level that he left it.

The next morning, he went to describe his experience to Ferlinghetti, who had news that worsened Kerouac's mood. Gabrielle had written Kerouac in care of Ferlinghetti's City Lights bookstore to tell him that his cat had died. Kerouac was shocked and sobbed as if he were reliving the death of his brother. Ferlinghetti was put off by the show of violent emotion and, believing that Kerouac was getting ready to go off on another drinking binge, advised him to go back to the cabin to get his head together.

Instead Kerouac set out on an epic drinking spree. First he met Philip Whalen for a drink just a door down from Ferlinghetti's store. Whalen wasn't a drinker, though, and, after seeing the effect that booze was having on Kerouac, decided to call it an early night. He handed Kerouac off to a more experienced drinker, Lou Welch. Kerouac had become close friends with Welch the year before, when Welch had driven him cross-country. Welch and Kerouac actually had much in common—an inordinate love for drink, a strange, convoluted relationship with their mothers, and an inability to have any sort of lasting relationship with women.

Together the two of them tore off drunkenly into the night to find Cassady. Kerouac was still nursing a deep guilt about not going to see Cassady in jail. It had been three years since they had seen each other, and Jack was outrageously drunk and beginning to get obnoxious. At the Cassadys' house, Jack shoved Carolyn, and Neal, still stinging at Kerouac's refusal to visit him and Kerouac's showing up so violently intoxicated, had little to say to him. The friendship was not renewed as Kerouac had hoped it might be. The group spent the night at the Cassadys', Kerouac sleeping outside, and in the morning he was contrite and apologetic.

The next day, Cassady asked a hungover and guilt-ridden Kerouac for a $100 loan for a mortgage payment. Kerouac immediately agreed (although the night before he had waved a handful of money in Carolyn's face, sneering, "That's the only reason people like me"), gathered as many friends as possible, and took off for Ferlinghetti's cabin for what turned into another three-day oceanside bender. While drunk, Kerouac arranged log-chopping contests and showed everyone the special way he had developed to unscrew wine jugs. When night fell, Kerouac stayed up reading from *Dr. Jekyll and Mr. Hyde*. In the mineral springs, where he bathed with his clothes on, Kerouac hallucinated giant toothed sperm coming to attack him. Kerouac consoled himself with another bottle of port and woke up the next morning in a feverish hangover of self-loathing.

He committed himself to drying out again in Ferlinghetti's cabin and managed for a while. Days later, when Neal and Carolyn came to visit and smoke marijuana with him, Kerouac admitted, reluctantly and sadly, that he hadn't written any prose in years. The pot started to make him paranoid and jealous of anyone who talked to Carolyn. Struck by his sadness and the mess that he was, she invited him to come live with her and Neal in Los Gatos. Kerouac agreed but upon accompanying them back to civilization began drinking immediately.

When Neal offered him his current girlfriend, Jacky, Kerouac agreed and then spent a week in her apartment, drinking wine, having sex, and slowly falling into a full-fledged breakdown. When friends visited him at Jacky's, they found Kerouac unable or unwilling to move from the armchair, rambling endlessly about conspiracy theories and drinking bottle after bottle of wine. Meanwhile Jacky, according to Tom Clark, became convinced that Jack was going to marry her and began to leak her "secret" to publicists, including gossip columnist (and thorn in Kerouac's side) Herb Caen.[6] Finally spurred on by a vision of Jacky's seven-year-old son's goldfish, which Kerouac had killed by filling its bowl with sweet port wine instead of water, he insisted that they leave Los Gatos and head back to Ferlinghetti's cabin. Jack called his trusty drunken chauffeur Welch, and the five of them (including Welch's girlfriend) headed out.

The next day, Kerouac realized that he had come without booze, and the gathering darkness descended. His hands trembled uncontrollably.

Jacky's son's questions tried his patience. The fact that he and Jacky often made love in front of the boy now disgusted Jack, and he soon convinced himself that Jacky was a witch attempting to harm him. The boy continued bothering Jack, and Jacky beat the boy until he was screaming, she was crying, and Jack was horrified. Jack became aware of camera-toting tourists wandering about and became convinced that they had poured kerosene into the creek to poison him. Screaming, he ran pell-mell from the cabin to the creek while his friends tried to calm him down. He became convinced that Neal had sent them to poison him to get his money. He sat in the corner and cried for his mother, sobbing that Welch and the rest of them were communists sent to ruin him. He had visions of the crucifix and demons. As dawn broke, the image of his dead cat filled his mind, and he began screaming and sobbing again. In the morning they drove him back to San Francisco, where he avoided his publisher, who told him he had to enter a sanatorium immediately. Ferlinghetti, however, perhaps realizing that it might be too late for Kerouac, told him to go home to his mother and move back to Lowell. Kerouac avoided everyone, then jumped on a jet on September 7 to go back to his mother. He had submerged his problems and his solutions, and they had grown too big for him to handle. He had not written in years. It was, in all respects, the beginning of the end.

Back in Northport, Kerouac continued drinking and worked, via mail, with Ferlinghetti to publish his dream journals (during the process, when the publisher had suggested changes in line breaks, Kerouac had confided to Ferlinghetti that he now believed himself to be a channel of God and that his writing was scripture and must be printed exactly as he had written it).

More and more, though, Kerouac began to understand that he had painted himself into a corner with his writing and his lifestyle, and that he was in the middle of a steep decline. He began looking for any way out. He told Ed White that he wished he was able to attend architectural school with him. When his friend Matsumi Kanemitsu began working at Lee Strasberg's famous actors' studio in midtown Manhattan, Kerouac asked for help in being enrolled there.

It was, like almost everything Kerouac tried at this point in his life, an unmitigated disaster. Strasberg, like so many other famous artistic types, was pleased to meet with Kerouac. Kerouac began to feel bored and antsy within 15 minutes and asked why he couldn't get a drink during the interview. He wandered around the building, hoping to find Marlon Brando. Matsumi begged Jack not to make a fool of himself by asking Brando for an autograph. Instead Kerouac asked Brando to go get a drink with him, but Brando refused. Jack hunted down Marilyn Monroe, who was taking classes at the studio, and when introduced, he said, "I like your legs!" Monroe stormed off in a huff. Jack made his way to the Cedar Bar, and the transformation that overtook him when drinking was obvious. At first he effused about Marilyn, sounding like a starstruck kid. But as more and more alcohol seeped into his system, he dramatically changed gears, denigrating the actress—the most pleasant thing he called her was a "trash broad."[7]

In January 1961, still trying to cure his alcoholism, he met Ginsberg at Timothy Leary's apartment to take LSD. Unprepared for the powerful reaction, Kerouac came out of the trip still an alcoholic, but sadder and more introspective than ever before. For years afterward he told everyone he knew that Leary was a liar, that the effects of LSD were long lasting, and that he had never been right after taking it.

Tortured by insomnia and hallucinations, Kerouac continued to distance himself from all his friends. One night in February, on a rare visit to his home by Ginsberg, when Kerouac's mother opined that "Hitler should have finished the job [on the Jews]," Jack sounded off in agreement. He wrote to Ferlinghetti angrily denouncing him, claiming nothing but hatred for him because of his publisher's trip to communist Cuba. In October 1961, Kerouac wrote Carolyn Cassady that he was "so sick and tired of being insulted by the Jew Talk of critics." He was convinced that there was a Jewish conspiracy against him and that the critics would only give good reviews to "their Philip Roths and Herbert Golds and Bernard Malamuds and J. D. Salingers and Saul Bellowses."[8] Now when Kerouac and his mother fought, they used the language not of young lovers but of people trapped in a brutal marriage—their arguments throbbed with the obscene and scatological insults they hurled at each other.

In spite of their deteriorating relationship, in May 1961 the two of them moved to Orlando, Florida, to be with Jack's sister. Once wooded, the lots that Kerouac found there disappointed him when he found them to be mostly denuded of trees and full of tract housing and a subdivision. Still, he found joy in helping around the house, by pointedly not writing, and by listening to the wind in the trees at night.

While he was there, fame found him again, but this time Kerouac was glad to have it. Literary criticism, in the form of doctoral theses, was being written about him. Granville Jones's thesis put Kerouac in the literary company of luminaries such as Walt Whitman and Herman Melville. French Canadian Bernice Lemire wrote a biographical thesis on Kerouac that (albeit unpublished) still stands as the only piece of critical biography to which Kerouac himself contributed while he was alive.

Jack lasted two months in the affluent subdivision where his sister lived and then headed off to Mexico again. Gathering the last bit of his energy and discipline, he began work again on *Desolation Angels*. *Desolation Angels* is also interesting because it was written in two parts. Book 1 was the last important work that Kerouac had written before the tempest of fame struck him, forcing him further and further inside himself and into the bottle. Depressingly enough, after *The Dharma Bums*, Kerouac would write no other substantial works other than finishing *Desolation Angels*.

Desolation Angels does a good job at depicting the 1950s America that Kerouac found himself living in, the "life in a fire lookout's shack, an evening at the Seattle burlesque, the North Beach coffeehouse-poetry reading coterie, the dreary circuit of bars, parties, and fruitless introductions that was and may always be fame in New York."[9] And yet there are large chunks of the book that are nonsense for nonsense's sake, and while critics have suggested that the nonsense is there to provide a mocking counterpoint to the beginning of what would become the overwhelming media blitz that constructs American culture today, it remains for the reader to decide if these chunks are carefully crafted social commentary or filler produced by a writer whose talents were waning. The book, like many of Kerouac's books, lacks a center, but one of the major changes here is the lack of a pair—while so many other books had buddies who worked together to find "IT," in *Desolation Angels*, the narrator finds himself alone against the world and is uncomfortable about it.

One of the book's overwhelming themes is that of change. There's a sense of overwhelming change, of change taking control of the narrator's life and a lack of power to stop or at least to influence the direction of change. Kerouac refers to the Bible, to Dante, to the American frontier, and, of course, to death. Unable to completely leave his Buddhist studies behind, Kerouac ends with the concept of the change of death leading to enlightenment. It's an ironic autobiographical statement coming from a man who had distanced himself from all his friends and from society at large and was doing his best to kill himself through alcohol abuse.

In Mexico, so lonely that he befriended a group of low-level thieves and hustlers and then watched placidly, drunk and stoned, as they stole everything he had brought with him—money, knife, flashlight, toiletries—except his raincoat, he thought about leaving for California. But he was sick and depressed. Instead he packed up the manuscript of *Desolation Angels* as well as a series of poems that he was calling "Cerrada Medellin Blues" and a huge supply of speed and sleeping pills and left for Florida.

There, in the fall, he returned to serious drinking—a full fifth of Johnnie Walker per day. He began telling people that writing was meaningless and that he was through with it, and yet just a few weeks after his return to Florida in early September, he once again took a handful of Benzedrine and sat down to write in ten days the story of his alcoholic stupor of the previous summer in California, calling it *Big Sur*. Unlike the rambling nature of *Desolation Angels*, *Big Sur* is distinct and noticeable because of its tight structure and compression of time and events. The book also marks Kerouac's discarding of the religious philosophy that filled his earlier books. He refers to his main character (again a thinly disguised autobiographical mask) as Jack Duluoz and suggests that he is a "Bhikku" and a "Bodhisattva" and also makes reference to the Christian religion. It's hard for many readers who have the idea of the thin, excited Jack speeding across the country to come to terms with the alcoholic, broken-down Jack who serves as the main character in *Big Sur*. In the end, the book is nothing more than a how-to book for alcoholic survival. It is one of the saddest books Kerouac ever wrote.

When he finished it, even though he had just finished recounting the story of his alcoholic collapse, he bought a case of cognac and drank straight for two weeks. By the time he was done, he was in the hospital. Checking out, he realized that he had no idea what had happened during his binge, and he sunk into an even-deeper depression. He had pushed things too long—no longer would his friends return his letters, and he had alienated his family, as well. He wrote Ferlinghetti saying that he was done writing.

Big Sur serves as a bookend to *On the Road*. It's telling that the Kerouac character suffers the same difficulties hitchhiking at the end of *Big Sur* as he does at the beginning of *On the Road*. At the end of *Big Sur*, Duluoz waits for hours without getting a ride and then is forced to walk on blistered feet. Drivers zoom past him, and he begins to realize that the world is a very different place than it was when *On the Road* was published, let alone from the time it was written.

Once again, the critics savaged Kerouac's work. Of *Big Sur*, the *Time* reviewer said that Kerouac was nothing more than a "perpetual adolescent." Herb Gold in the *Saturday Review* said that Kerouac so far had produced nothing but a "flood of trivia." Even Ferlinghetti was not pleased with the new book. He took exception to being portrayed as a genial businessman and felt that Jack was trying to blame his cabin or the locale for his problems, which Ferlinghetti said were nothing more than the result of drinking too much sweet wine.

Other than bad reviews, Jack had long since fallen out of the media altogether, and it was only a court case that brought him back into it. In March 1962, he was called out of his drunken stupor to a New York City courtroom to settle in family court the matter of the child he had fathered with Joan Haverty more than a decade before. This time Kerouac took a blood test, which revealed that Janet Michelle could possibly be his daughter (at the time, the test was not accurate enough to reveal a 100 percent answer). Jack went out to lunch with the girl and her mother but was awkward around her, fascinated with seeing himself replicated in miniature, female form. Still, however, Kerouac denied paternity. Finally the judge made Kerouac a deal—acknowledge that he was the father of the girl, and he would only have to pay the minimum amount of child support, $52 a month. Kerouac accepted reluctantly and then left the city angry, complaining that the legal fees he had spent on the case had used up the last of his money, plunging him and his mother back into poverty.

Upon his return to Florida in March, he was greeted with the good news that *Big Sur* and, perhaps most importantly to Kerouac, *Visions of Gerard* had both been sold to Farrar, Straus and Cudahy. But bad news also greeted him in Florida—heavier than he had ever been, he was uncomfortable in the heat and the humidity. Marital tensions between his sister and brother-in-law were at an all-time high. Paul was no longer attempting to even pretend to hide his infidelity. He would leave his wife and child, Paul Jr., for six months at a time to stay with his mistress. In addition, the balance of resentment had shifted. While Paul at one point had hated Jack and his work-shirking and hard-drinking ways, now it was Paul who owed Kerouac $5,000, money that was never to be repaid. In addition, Paul Jr. idolized his uncle Jack to the point of preferring his company over that of his father.

By summertime, Kerouac was trying to avoid the heat by spending his time drinking whiskey in the air-conditioning. However, the endless alcohol abuse pushed him to another breaking point. Nicosia relates a shocking story: "Since Paul, Sr., was out of town, Jack told Paul to take him for a ride in his father's Sprite. At fourteen Paul only had a learner's permit, but he was reassured by his uncle's bravado. As they passed the brick wall that separated the black neighborhoods from the rest of Orlando, Jack blustered, 'You ought to go burn a cross up there!' After they returned home he helped Paul build a cross with two by fours, and at night they drove back to the wall, covered the cross with cloth, and saturated it with kerosene. After erecting it on the wall and lighting it, Jack started yelling obscenities."[10]

In late summer of 1962, Kerouac and his mother decided to move back to New England, but Kerouac could find nowhere that he wanted stay— in Maine he was beaten senseless by nightclub bouncers offended by his vicious racist slurs. He nursed his wounds on trains and buses before finally ending up in the house of John Clellon Holmes in Old Saybrook, Connecticut, on September 9, 1962. There Kerouac was paralyzed by alcohol again. A week passed without him bathing or shaving. The only time he stirred from his brandy and easy chair and television was when dinner was served. He spent afternoons passed out in the chair, only waking to refill his glass. Holmes said that Kerouac would rant and claim to be at various times Christ, Satan, a genius, and an Indian chief. Finally, humiliated at appearing this way in front of his (once-again) friend and family, Kerouac poured himself a Mason jar full of brandy and hired a car to take him to Lowell.

In Lowell, Kerouac outdid himself with a 20-day drinking spree, alienating almost everyone with whom he came in contact. He showed up first at the home of his childhood friend G. J. Apostolos. Times had changed, though, and father and husband Apostolos was in no position to party with Kerouac, especially when Jack frightened Mrs. Apostolos by dancing on top of the family's piano. When asked to appear on a local radio show called *Dialogues in Great Books*, Kerouac showed up incoherently drunk, raving a monologue about Gerard, his childhood, his mystical faith, and his belief that Gerard was, in a sense, his personal angel, guiding and controlling him.

His drinking was so severe that the alcoholic blackouts came faster and closer together—he wrote friends duplicate letters because he couldn't remember that he had already written them. He was destroyed when one of the letters in return informed him that Neal and Carolyn Cassady were contemplating divorce.

The only good thing that happened in Lowell was the reunion between Kerouac and the Sampas family. Tony Sampas was Kerouac's old friend Sammy's younger brother. A nervous, well-educated, but decidedly working-class man, Tony—and his sister Stella—were saddened by Kerouac's state and immediately took it upon themselves to watch over him.

While Kerouac was in Lowell, *Big Sur* came out. The reviews were uneven, but he shrugged them off. With the big swing toward Jewish lit, which was awarding writers like J. D. Salinger and Saul Bellow critical acclaim, Kerouac told anyone who would listen that it was all part of the Jewish conspiracy against him. Finally, exhausted, he flew back to Florida, sold his home there, collected his mother and their cats, and moved back to Northport on Christmas Eve, 1962. Once again, he attempted to keep his address secret from all but his closest friends. There he began to work, painfully slowly, on a new book he was calling *Vanity of Duluoz*.

Jack was slowly cutting off the few friends that still tried to keep in touch with him. When Gary Snyder sent Kerouac a Japanese college student's thesis on *The Subterraneans*, in which she attempted to psychoanalyze the author through the text of the book, Kerouac sent back a vile, hate-filled letter describing all the different ways he hated women for their seductive ways, and also dragged Ginsberg and even Snyder into the mix, calling him a Zen heretic. Snyder responded with a kind letter, but Kerouac refused to ever contact him again.

Kerouac found locals to pal around with on Long Island, including the painter Stanley Twardowicz, but was too drunk to do much of anything. Nicosia relates stories of softball games that Kerouac's Northport friends would drag him to, simply to get him out of the house, Kerouac dressed in slippers. Too drunk to catch fly balls, he did somersaults in the outfield. When the once-national-class athlete fell going for a fly ball and passed out, he woke up two innings later and shouted his encouragement to keep the game going—unaware that he had been unconscious.

In late July 1963, Neal showed up at Kerouac's new Northport home, as he had so many times in their young adulthood. This time there was a difference. After putting up with everything—the wild open infidelity, the drugs, the lack of jobs, the prison sentences—Carolyn had finally had enough and divorced Neal. Kerouac was displeased with the whole situation, and unlike in the past, he put up with a cursory visit and then sent Neal on his way, not joining him.

In September 1963, *Visions of Gerard* was published. The critics called it nostalgic and syrupy sweet. Saul Maloff of the *New York Times* (the newspaper that had kick-started Kerouac's career so many years ago) wrote that the book was "bathos of the most lachrymose kind... [and] accused Jack of 'betraying' and 'debasing' Gerard's suffering with his 'garrulous hipster yawping.' "[11]

In March 1964, Kerouac was asked to read at Harvard by a group of students from Lowell House who were entranced by the lucky coincidence of the names. Kerouac dreaded all readings at this point in his life and knew that he was becoming a public embarrassment because of his drinking. However, he was always needy of acceptance, and the lure of reading at Harvard was too much to resist.

He was drunk the entire time he was there. When he was supposed to read, he was already so drunk that he couldn't read and fell constantly. He sketched on napkins and made anti-Semitic jokes. The students thought it howlingly funny and continued feeding him drinks and goading him into more and more extreme rants, against communism and the Chinese. The newspaper photos the next day showed a fat, drunken buffoon.

The embarrassment that he suffered was not enough to convince him to leave. Already far outstaying his welcome, he stayed in the room that had been provided for him until eventually the school administration ordered him to leave. When he arrived home, he found that his mother had already put their Northport home up for sale and was preparing to move her son and his household back to Florida.

In the summer of 1964, as Kerouac was making arrangements to move back to Florida, a ghost from his past showed up at his door once again. Neal Cassady had been an important link between the Beats and the hippies and was one of the few Beats to accept and embrace the attention of the 1960s counterculture. Neal was now driving a restored school bus named Furthur for Ken Kesey's group of acid-taking hippies, the Merry Pranksters. Kerouac had enjoyed reading Kesey's *One Flew over the Cuckoo's Nest*, but now he greeted the Pranksters with cold stares. Jack's deep social conservatism now surrounded him like a comfortable blanket. He didn't like these kids and thought of them as disrespectful, as careless, as living up to all the traits that the media had attempted to affix to him and that he had fought so hard against. Kerouac was disappointed in Cassady for joining in.

Prison, drugs, and womanizing had not been kind to Neal. The unlimited speed and acid had changed his personality deeply. He was angrier, harder, less open and honest. Kerouac felt that he had empty, dead eyes.

It didn't matter to Kesey. He wanted to meet Jack. Jack was unsure about meeting Kesey, but he agreed to show up at one of their parties. By the time he got there, they had all dropped acid. Kerouac was aghast that they were using an American flag as decoration. He carefully folded it and put it aside, to the derision of the Pranksters. In just a few minutes, Kerouac, Kesey, and Cassady all realized that bringing Jack there had been a mistake.

NOTES

1. Jonathan Paul Eburne, "Trafficking in the Void: Burroughs, Kerouac, and the Consumption of Otherness," *Modern Fiction Studies* 43, no. 1 (1997): p. 58.

2. Gerald Nicosia, *Memory Babe* (Berkeley: University of California Press, 1994), p. 610.

3. Jack Kerouac, *Selected Letters, 1957–1969* (New York: Viking, 1999), p. 441.

4. Kerouac, *Selected Letters, 1957–1969*, p. 9.

5. Jack Kerouac, *Book of Dreams*, (San Francisco: City Light Books, 1961), p. 3.

6. Tom Clarke, *Jack Kerouac*, (New York: Thunder's Mouth Press, 2001), p. 182.

7. Nicosia, *Memory Babe*, p. 624.

8. Kerouac, *Selected Letters, 1957–1969*, p. 308.

9. Nicosia, *Memory Babe*, p. 624.

10. Nicosia, *Memory Babe*, p. 634.

11. Nicosia, *Memory Babe*, p. 648.

Chapter 15

DEATH

By 1964, Kerouac's work was out of print. In August 1964, fed up with the visitors, not only Cassady but scores of drunken high school and college students who showed up at the Northport home looking for Dean Moriarty and finding a lonely, potbellied drunk instead, Kerouac and his mother packed up and moved again, this time to Saint Petersburg, Florida.

On September 19, 1964, Jack was coming home from the bars when his mother met him at the door sobbing. Jack's sister Carolyn was dead. Her husband, Paul, had left her and moved in with his mistress. Carolyn, overworked trying to make enough money to support her and her son, Paul Jr., had lost so much weight that at the time of her death she barely weighed 90 pounds. Nin had died of a heart attack brought on by the shock of her husband calling her on the phone to ask for a divorce. Kerouac was devastated again and sought solace in even more drinking. After the funeral, he busied himself with the prepublication galleys of *Desolation Angels*.

Desolation Angels is another circular narrative, much like *On the Road*—beginning and ending with the disturbing image of a man confronting what he finds within himself. His time spent on the mountain serves only to make him realize how much the terrors of his outer world—thunderstorms, gorges, thick fog—reflect the mess that his interior life has become. At the end of the book, he descends from the mountain believing that "a peaceful sorrow at home is the best I'll ever be able to offer the world."

Unfortunately, once again, the critics did not agree. Saul Maloff's review in the *New York Times* (May 2, 1965) had more to do with his dislike of Kerouac as a person than with Kerouac's writing. Charles Poore, also in the *New York Times*, put another nail in Kerouac's coffin by suggesting that the book was nothing more than an artifact from a vanished culture. Nelson Algren, a fellow traveler and author of cultish books such as *The Man with the Golden Arm*, wrote that "Kerouac's prose is not prose; it is a form of self-indulgence."[1]

This time, however, Kerouac didn't take the beatings with a bowed head as he usually did. Instead he took a step that he had been considering for some time—he began to think about a serious critical defense of his work.

However, his plans were slowed by his lack of self-control. His drinking continued, and he spent a night in jail for public urination. Again, the reviewers of *Desolation Angels* were savage. Fleeing the poison-pen jabs, he headed for France, arriving in Paris in July 1965.

In France, he drank, bought the services of whores, and once, when he felt threatened, managed to cut himself opening his Swiss army knife to fight off imagined attackers. He went to the Bibliothèque Nationale to research his genealogy, only to find that the records had been burned by the Nazis, and so he returned to the bars. His paranoia seethed. He believed that the French police were deliberately giving him wrong directions, and that every citizen he met was planning to mug him. He felt incredibly isolated and lonely without his mother, and once, while resting outside a church, he was mistaken for a homeless man. Originally he had hoped to write a second part to his "Sea" poem, this time concentrating on the sounds of the Atlantic off the coast of Brittany. By the time he got there, though, he had misplaced his pencils and notebooks. Instead he hunted down a man to whom he thought he might be related and, after several drinks, decided they were indeed cousins. Taking the train to Brest, he drunkenly lectured a priest on religion, drank for eight hours, and returned to Paris and the airplane back to Florida.

In a week, Kerouac had burned through $1,500, mostly in bars. After flying home, still drinking heavily, he typed out a chronicle of his trip in about a week and entitled it *Satori in Paris*. The alcohol was taking a harsh toll on his writing, and the book is sloppy and uneven. Although the thesis of the book is that he achieved some sort of revelation in his drunken debauches, it is difficult for the reader, without using a great deal of imagination, to determine exactly where that enlightenment may have occurred. In fact, Charters suggests that Kerouac saw every moment of the trip as a satori, or enlightenment or knowing oneself. It may be that he was so lonely, so starved for human contact other than his mother, that every time he spoke to someone it was a delight, a little miracle.

Separated into 38 sections, *Satori in Paris* ignores Kerouac's losing strug-gle with alcoholism—there's plenty of drinking in it, but no ill effects. Kerouac drinks beer for breakfast and cognac by the gallon, but the results that we know really happened, the paranoia and the failed encounters with women, are either glossed over or played for laughs. For example, when the librarians of the Bibliothèque Nationale refuse to bring him the books he needs to research his family's history because they worry about the safety of the books in the hands of a shabbily dressed man who reeks of alcohol, he attacks them for their small-mindedness. It's a strange omis-sion for a writer who took on his alcoholism so honestly in *Big Sur*. In addition, the writing itself seems a movement away from Kerouac's spon-taneous prose experimentation in texts like *Visions of Cody* and a return to the more straightforward writing of *The Dharma Bums*.

By section 14, Kerouac is already complaining about being homesick and consoles himself again and again with more cognac. Deciding to take a plane to Brittany to continue the research into his family tree, he misses his flight when he leaves the airport to look for a toilet. Forced to take a train, he begins drinking with a French soldier and before long finds him-self drunkenly confronting a priest to explain his philosophy of Christian-ity, which he adds might have been his moment of satori. However, it's a cabdriver who drives him to the airport and delivers a monologue about the importance of family that Kerouac finally identifies as his probable moment of satori, or enlightenment; but it's difficult for the reader to make that leap, and in the end, the book feels slightly sad, vaguely misog-ynistic, and highly self-indulgent.

Once again, Kerouac felt that the time had come to move. He sold his house and headed to Hyannis, on Cape Cod, and bought a house. Kerouac and his mother moved to Cape Cod in May 1966, closer to Tony Sampas and his sister Stella, both of whom visited regularly.

For a month Kerouac did nothing but drink, sleep, and listen to jazz. He had promised his Italian publishers that he would fly over to make some public appearances to support his book sales in that country; however, comfortable in his new home, he continued to postpone the trip. It was here that Kerouac started to cultivate his phone habit. It seemed that now, after pushing people away for so long, he could not stand not to talk to them. Hopelessly drunk, he would attempt to keep friends and relatives on the phone for hours, and the bills were crushing.

Later that summer Ann Charters, future Beat authority, then a Colum-bia graduate student, began visiting with Kerouac to compile a complete bibliography of his work. Knowing exactly how to play the Kerouac game, she wrote to his mother first, telling her that she had been asked to compile a bibliography of all Kerouac's work by the Phoenix Bookstore in New York City. Kerouac was pleased but wary; kids still dropped by looking for the hero of *On the Road*. Kerouac told Charters that one of the worst moments of his life was when a group of teens with jackets lettered "dharma bums" came by his home, and instead of the vibrant 20-something they expected to find, a drunk, rumpled, fat, red-faced man opened the door. Their faces fell, and Kerouac was too embarrassed and saddened to do anything but shut the door. Eventually Kerouac agreed to let Charters look at his personal archives, with the admonishment that she would have to be a perfect gentlewoman so as not to incur his mother's wrath. He also asked her to bring the directions that he sent her to his home, so that he could destroy them himself, in an effort to keep his whereabouts a little more private.

Kerouac drank steadily the entire time, but Charters was impressed with how carefully he had kept everything through all the years of travel. Later in the afternoon, Kerouac took Charters for a drive in his car, discussing his support for the war in Vietnam and sipping booze continually. Returning to the Kerouac house, they ate dinner, and she thanked Jack and Gabrielle for their hospitality, saying that she was off to her hotel but would be back tomorrow to finish her work.

Suddenly Kerouac attempted to draw Charters into the surrealistic alcoholic drama that had become his life. He wanted her to spend the night with him, he said, adding that he would refuse to finish the project unless she had sex with him. When Charters refused, he left to use the bathroom. While he was gone, Gabrielle grabbed Charters's arm and led her out, showing her a hole in the wall where she said that Jack had thrown a knife at her. Kerouac came out of the bathroom and started yelling at his mother for showing Charters the hole. She yelled back, and while they were screaming at each other, Charters made her getaway, with Kerouac following her outside, yelling for her to come back.

On September 9, 1966, Kerouac's mother suffered a stroke, paralyzing her almost completely. Jack was wracked with feelings of guilt because he had been out in the bars while his mother lay stricken, naked on the bathroom floor, for hours. Wracked with guilt and fear, Kerouac fussed for weeks. Finally things came to a head when his Italian publisher called again and insisted that he live up to his agreement. He called Stella Sampas (who had been visiting them on and off throughout the summer) and asked her to take care of his mother while he was gone.

Again, he turned to drink. By the time his flight got to London, he was so drunk that he had to be carried off the plane. In Italy, he had an attack of hysteria and was injected with morphine by an Italian doctor to calm him—but the opposite effect was realized as Kerouac, deep in paranoia, believed that evil dark forces were out to kill him. Kerouac passed out repeatedly when his translator, whom he would later call a "Russian Jewish Communist spy," took him out to dinner. He guzzled champagne and complained that with his mother being in the condition that she was, he needed someone to take care of her, so that he would be forced to go back on his promise to himself and get married again.

On November 18, 1966, Kerouac and Stella Sampas were married by a justice of the peace at Jack's home. Stella told people that she had fallen in love with Jack the first time he had come over to meet her brother as a teen. She also told people that she was still a virgin and had saved herself for Jack all those years since she had developed a high school crush on Jack Kerouac the football star.

In January 1967, Jack, Gabrielle, and Stella moved back to Lowell. Here Jack had a smaller chance of being arrested for drunk and disorderly behavior—which had become a common occurrence on the Cape. Here he could drink in Nicky's, a bar owned by one brother-in-law and managed by another, Tony. Stella may have been an odd woman, but she cared for Gabrielle Kerouac as if she was her own mother. Stella also attempted to press some order into Jack's life, trying to force him to write from nine to five and sending her brothers out to retrieve him from the bars. Stella took to hiding his shoes to try to keep him home and out of the bars, but Kerouac simply went out barefoot. She also disconnected the phone—Kerouac's drunkenly long-winded long-distance conversations with Carolyn Cassady were crushing them with bills.

Nicosia writes that when he went to Lowell to interview people who knew Kerouac during this period in his life, he found story after story of a drunken, debauched, friendless man who had become the butt of jokes and had earned a reputation as a rummy: "His former best friends, like G. J. Apostolos, would cross the street to avoid meeting him. His vile language in front of women caused several old friends to punch him and throw him out of their bars. He was even thrown out of the Pawtucketville Social Club, which his father had once managed. People complained that he 'stank like a goat'; they laughed that the great author was often to be found passed out under a pinball machine. Those close to him barely tolerated him. Most people did not understand him at all, and out of sheer loneliness and boredom he chose the company of barflies, bartenders, bums and minor criminals."[2]

In the spring of 1967, Kerouac wrote what would be his last work, *Vanity of Duluoz*. Much has been made about the autobiographical content of the book, the idea that it is a man writing to his new wife, trying to explain why he is the way he is. The book sprawls from his teenage football stardom up to the point where he is thrust into the world of fame.

The book is divided into 13 sections, or books, and each one describes a season in his life. In the book, he dismisses a good deal of his previous work. He (as narrator) laughs not only at his earlier writing but at his adoption of Buddhism as well. He talks about how he is too sensitive and that he has been hurt repeatedly by believing too much in others.

The book itself was finished in mid-May and was due at the publishers a month later. However, he was drinking so much that he had difficulty making the revisions needed before sending it off to the publisher.

Meanwhile his drinking was also making his home life impossible. His mother refused to take any therapy or spend any time in the hospital. After being in control for so long, she found it impossible to give away any of the power in "her" home. Jack and Stella began fighting. She dumped booze on his head and tore the phone out of the wall. He threw chairs at her. Her family attempted to give him some sort of support system, welcoming him into the family. Although Jack was touched, he was recognizing that it was too late for him. That fall, when three interviewers from the *Paris Review* came by to talk to him, Kerouac candidly admitted, "Frankly, I do feel my mind is going."[3]

Money was a constant problem as well. Although *Vanity of Duluoz* had been sold, as well as several small magazine articles, the new mortgage and his mother's medical bills drained his finances. Kerouac was offered and accepted a position as a writer in residence at Lowell Tech, but when the first day of class came, Kerouac was blind drunk and spat obscenities at everyone with whom he came in contact.

He sneaked around Mary Carney's (the woman who inspired *Maggie Cassidy*) house, frightening her. He took trips into Manhattan and picked up whores with whom he was unable to perform. He tossed down a quart of Johnnie Walker every day and chased it with can after can of beer.

It seemed unlikely that anyone could survive the drinking that Jack was undertaking. In early February 1968, Carolyn Cassady called on the now-connected phone to tell Jack that Neal had been found dead in Mexico, felled by a combination of drugs, alcohol, and heat. Stella refused to pass on the message. The next day when Carolyn called, she talked directly to Jack, who refused to believe the news.

Nicosia describes a visit by the writer Gregory McDonald to the Kerouac household. McDonald felt that he was watching a man self-destruct before his very eyes. Kerouac was drinking an average of 14 boilermakers an hour from morning until night. He was in no condition for another move, but his mother insisted, telling him that the climate change would be good for both of them. Low on funds and on inspiration, Kerouac was unable to act on the request immediately.

To dull the pain of his loss of Cassady (about whom Jack had begun to obsess), he made a poorly planned trip to Europe that he couldn't afford, stumbling drunk through the streets chaperoned by Tony Sampas, and hiring whores with whom he couldn't perform. Kerouac returned to the United States more depressed than ever.

In the fall of 1968, he was invited to appear on *Firing Line* with William F. Buckley. By this time the hippie movement was in full swing in America, and although most of them admitted that they drew their inspiration from Kerouac and the rest of the Beat writers, Kerouac wanted nothing to do with them. From his books, the public expected him to be as seemingly goofy as Ginsberg, but instead, with his far-right politics, his anti-Semitism, and his racism, Kerouac was much closer to the average rural John Bircher. The show was a disaster, but what was important was that, after being driven down to New York City, Kerouac found himself for the first time since 1953 in the company of Ginsberg, Burroughs, and Corso. In Burroughs's hotel room, they reminisced, and Burroughs warned Kerouac, rightly so, about appearing on Buckley's TV program. Kerouac couldn't be dissuaded, though, and left Burroughs's apartment with Ginsberg, whom he begged to come along for moral support. Kerouac also picked up a pint of scotch and guzzled it on the way to the TV studio. Buckley was disgusted by Kerouac's drunken mumblings, and Kerouac passed out several times, nodding off in his chair. He forgot his fellow panelists' names. During the show, another panelist linked Ginsberg and Kerouac. Kerouac responded angrily, saying, "I'm not connected with Ginsberg, and don't you put my name next to his." When the camera panned to Ginsberg in the audience, he revealed only a tender, bemused smile. Outside the studio after taping, Ginsberg said good-bye to Jack, ignoring his vicious outburst. It was the last time Ginsberg would see him alive.

Upon returning to Lowell, Kerouac decided, after his mother's strong suggestion, that they should move the family back to Saint Petersburg. He sold his correspondence with Ginsberg to Columbia University and made moves to immediately sell their Northport home, at a loss. Before they could finalize plans, though, there was another surprise from the past. Late in August, a hippie girl showed up at his door. Used to such unannounced visitors, Stella prepared to turn the girl away. When she heard what the girl had to say, though, Stella told her which bar Jack was drinking in that day. And so it was that Jack Kerouac met his daughter Janet Michelle Kerouac. He had nothing to say to her, other than giving her his blessing to use the family name. It seemed that he was settling accounts with all his old ghosts.

In Saint Petersburg, Kerouac was a veritable shut-in. Not even bothering to go to bars anymore, he drank at home, in the backyard. Looking up some of his old drinking buddies, Kerouac took a huge dose of LSD. Mentally, he couldn't deal. After coming down from his trip, he stayed in bed for six weeks, depressed and unable to recover.

Kerouac spent long hours in Florida drinking and playing the baseball game that he had invented as a child. The game, which is now on display with other Kerouac artifacts at the New York City Public Library, consists of six teams, named after automobiles (the Saint Louis Cadillacs, the Washington Chryslers, the Pittsburgh Plymouths), and a variety of players with typically colorful names (Wino Love, for instance). Kerouac kept detailed and copious records of his players, and the rules he developed himself were confusing as well—he threw an eraser onto the homemade board, and then, depending on what segment of the board the eraser landed in, he would refer to the back of the player's card to determine what moves would be made. Eventually he even wrote a short story about one of the players, "Ronnie on the Mound," which was never published.

Jack and Stella still fought, and although he had moments of tenderness, by the summer of 1969, he was convinced that she was trying to poison him. Behind her back, he began to make efforts to divorce her.

Knowing nothing of her husband's machinations, Stella soldiered on, taking care of her mother-in-law. Poverty was closing in on them, and in addition to taking care of Gabrielle night and day, Stella had gone to work as a part-time seamstress. Kerouac began working on a book entitled *Pic* in the summer of 1969. The story of a young African American, the book is wildly uneven.

Pic is Pictorial Review Jackson, an African American orphan whose life is turned upside down when his grandfather/caretaker is taken to the hospital. Pic, who gets shuffled off to his aunt's house, is rescued by his older brother Slim. Slim and Pic take off across the country hitchhiking to find a new home in California. Unbelievably, at the end of the book, the boys are saved by an Irish Catholic priest who discovers that Pic can sing and offers him a place to live and a job singing in the church.

In Kerouac's first ending of *Pic*, he had the main characters meet up with Dean and Sal from *On the Road*. Stella objected, and Kerouac stormed off, asking his mother how it should end, and creating another ending in which the main characters instead wound up with the Ghost of the Susquehanna, also from *On the Road*, in a church. Curiously enough, Timothy Hunt, in *Kerouac's Crooked Road*, puts forth his theory that *Pic* is actually nothing more than a very early draft of *On the Road* to which Kerouac returned and edited when he was completely dried up as a writer. (Hunt also suggests that there were five drafts of On the Road overall: the first two unpublished, the third draft published as Pic, the fourth as On the Road, and the fifth as Visions of Cody.) Whatever the case, that he was asking and accepting advice from his mother on how to end his book suggests that Kerouac's powers as a writer were finished.[4]

Adding to the book's appearance of being wildly patched together for fast cash is the main character's dialect. Many Kerouac scholars believe that he was attempting to replicate the language and dialect that he heard while living with his sister in North Carolina; it is, however, dreadful: "ever'wherer I turn my ear I hear au-tos, and folkses talking and all kind of noises and music, I tell you, it was the noise of ever'body *doin something* at the same time all over with they hands and feet and voices, jess as plain."[5] The diction jumps back and forth between someone who does not sound like the majority of Kerouac's narrators and someone who sounds quite like a Kerouac narrator. The result is a disturbing, shuck-and-jive, minstrel-like accent that shows just how far Kerouac's reputed memory and his ability to capture language had fallen owing to his alcoholic deterioration. Foolishly, he went to an African American bar for a binge to celebrate finishing his book. Because of his graphic racism, before long the patrons beat him unconscious and left him in the parking lot.

Jack McClintock, a writer for *Esquire*, visited Kerouac toward the end of his life and collected the impressions he received in an article called "This Is How the Ride Ends" in March 1970. In it, McClintock expresses the sadness of seeing Kerouac as he was in his last years, so far from the youthful, excited man who had driven across the country in search of kicks. McClintock relates how Kerouac still refused to believe that Cassady was dead and blamed Ginsberg, Kesey, and the rest of the nascent hippie movement for ruining Neal, just as Neal's wife Carolyn would also claim in her book *Off the Road*.

Later in the summer of 1969, Kerouac had been so firmly planted in the "where are they now" category that the *Chicago Tribune*, when putting together a collection of fifties nostalgia, asked Kerouac to contribute. He did so, for $1,500 (money that he and his family sorely needed). That article, "After Me, The Deluge," was his final statement on his artistry and the Beat generation as a whole. In it he distanced himself from the current antiestablishment figures, including Ginsberg, Jerry Rubin, and Abbie Hoffman. Kerouac wrote that he now considered himself an "inconsolable orphan...yelling and screaming...to make arrangements for making a living yet all bespattered and gloomed-up in the night soil of poor body and soul...and all so lonered."[6]

On October 20, 1969, Kerouac was sitting in front of the TV, already drunk before noon. He was watching *The Galloping Gourmet* and eating a can of tuna fish when a vein in his stomach ruptured from years of heavy drinking and drug abuse. He was rushed to the hospital, where the doctors managed to keep him alive for 20 hours, until, at 5:30 A.M. on October 21, 1969, Jack Kerouac died.

After his death, the critics who had been so harsh to him turned out their words of kindness. On October 23, Kerouac's body arrived in Lowell, and the family was brought together for a wake. The funeral took place in the same spot where he had studied to be an altar boy in Saint Jean Baptiste Church. His old friend Father "Spike" Morrisette delivered the eulogy. Although when Charters wrote her groundbreaking biography of Kerouac in 1973, his grave was still unmarked, today his plot in Lowell's Edson Cemetery, in the Sampas family plot, is a place of pilgrimage for dharma bums from all over.

NOTES

1. Gerald Nicosia, *Memory Babe* (Berkeley: University of California Press, 1994), p. 625.

2. Nicosia, *Memory Babe*, p. 672.

3. Kerouac, quoted in Ann Charters, *Kerouac* (San Francisco: Straight Arrow Books, 1973), p. 365.

4. Ann Charters and Tim Hunt, *Kerouac's Crooked Road: Development of a Fiction* (Berkeley: University of California Press, 1996), p. 287.

5. Jack Kerouac, *Pic* (New York: Grove, 1971), p. 48.

6. Jack Kerouac, "After Me, The Deluge." *Chicago Tribune*, September 28 1969.

Chapter 16

LEGACY

While Stella Kerouac was alive, she kept an ironfisted control over Kerouac's archive, which he had collected his entire life. When Charters first contacted Kerouac about writing a bibliography of his work, he responded by letter, saying, "I've kept the neatest records you ever saw.... I'll just pull everything out one by one, hand them to you at the desk, return the things back where they were (innumerable poetry pamphlets, broadsides, sheets from magazine publications, etc.)."[1]

Kerouac also had hundreds upon hundreds of copies of his letters—both the ones he received and carbon copies of the ones he wrote. Ironically, Kerouac's marriage to Stella also expanded the archive, as her family kept all the letters that Kerouac wrote to her brother Sebastian while he was in World War II, before he was killed on the beaches of Anzio. Stella released few if any of Kerouac's unpublished works while he was alive, storing the voluminous boxes and files in a bank vault in Lowell. However, after her death, the new executor of the estate, John Sampas, took steps to make the archive more available to scholars interested in studying Kerouac's work as well as recovering Kerouac's unpublished or unfinished work.

Today the New York Public Library holds Kerouac's personal archive, consisting of more than 1,050 manuscripts and typescripts, including short stories, novels, prose pieces, poems, and fragments; 130 notebooks for almost all his works (both published and unpublished); 52 journals dating from 1934 to 1960, which include materials used in *The Town and the City*, *On the Road*, *Big Sur*, and other works; 55 diaries dating from 1956 to 1969; about 1,800 pieces of correspondence; 72 publishing contracts; and Kerouac's fantasy baseball game.

Gerald Nicosia's 1999 lawsuit against the Sampas family revealed that
Kerouac left thousands of pages of unpublished manuscripts, journals, and
letters that editors and publishers continue to sort through, which occa-
sionally see print. *Atop an Underwood* was published in 1999, *Orpheus
Emerged* came out in 2000 as an e-book, and Kerouac's letters, edited by
Anne Charters, are being released slowly and strategically.

Today there is a thriving industry in the release of Kerouac's previously
unpublished works. *Some of the Dharma* was one of the first books published after Kerouac's death and is different from many of the texts that
were published posthumously. Unlike *Atop an Underwood* or *Orpheus
Emerged*, *Some of the Dharma* is not a cobbled-together collection of stories from notebooks. Rather, it is a book that Kerouac had put together
but failed to find a publisher for during the period in which he was most
influenced by Buddhism. It includes not only poems but also notes, ideas,
stories, letter fragments, and dialogues, as well as journal entries and even
sketches that Kerouac had made in the margins of his journals.

One can make many assumptions about why *Some of the Dharma* was
never published during Kerouac's lifetime—certainly he was before his
time when it came to an interest and openness toward Eastern religions.
It is nonnarrative and experimental, a type of writing for which an audience had just begun to develop. The book, like so much of Kerouac's
work, is wildly uneven, and while there are moments of true clarity and
beauty, there are also the old Kerouacian problems of self-indulgence (ev-
ident in the lengthy discussion of what he saw at this point as his youthful failings, and his discussions about his losing battle with the alcoholism
that would eventually kill him) and misogyny. The book's comprehen-
siveness is double-edged. While it is valuable to Kerouac scholars because
its the unedited nature and rawness of thought, the book is prohibitive to
the general reader because of it tendency to collect every one of Kerouac's
stray thoughts on the minutiae of his life within Buddha.

Most critics agree that *Orpheus Emerged* is not one of the strongest posthumously published works. Kerouac wrote this during his first few years in New
York City, completing it in 1945. It is revealing that the plot, like Kerouac's
later, more celebrated work, is largely autobiographical, following the adventures of Columbia students and would-be poets who live according to a
set of ideals that they have created for themselves and now intend on living
through. They throw parties where they talk about their ideas and drink gallons of cheap wine. The book differentiates itself from Kerouac's later autobiographical work because of the stiff characters and awkward dialogue.[2]

What's interesting and new about the book is not the plot but the form
in which the book is published. This title was initially released electroni-

cally, and the book comes bundled with a CD-ROM containing the full text as well as a foreword, an introduction by Robert Creeley, a biography of Kerouac, a snippet from his *Lonesome Traveler*, and separate bibliographies.

Kerouac's *Book of Haikus* is another posthumously published text. This one collects what he called his haikus. These are not actual traditional haikus. According to Regina Weinreich, who wrote the foreword to *Book of Haikus*, Kerouac felt constrained by the classic Japanese haiku form and so invented his own form, calling it the American haiku, which, he wrote, should "simply say a lot in three short lines."[3] Some of these poems are collected from the notebooks that he carried with him everywhere. Weinreich also gathered examples of Kerouac's haikus from a variety of other places—journals, letters, and other writings.

Atop an Underwood was greeted (as was all Kerouac's work when he was alive) with mixed reviews. Many people felt that publishing the work, which was undeniably juvenilia, was nothing more than exhuming Kerouac's corpse for a few extra dollars. Others, however, suggested that the book was a valuable addition to Kerouac scholarship.

Atop an Underwood takes its name from a collection that Kerouac proposed in 1941. Kerouac had left a table of contents for the book, which outlined 66 stories in all. Typical of Kerouac, though, there were multiple copies of this table of contents; some had listed only 25 story titles, while others had 42, and still others 48. The editor of *Atop an Underwood* determined that out of all the stories listed, only 15 still existed, and the rest had been lost to time or had never existed as anything more than a title or fragment.

The book is set up in parts, in the style of Kerouac's later, more mature works. Part 1 covers the years from 1936 to 1940 and draws on the stories he wrote for the newspapers that he created for his own amusement and goes all the way to his first fall at Columbia University. Part 2 covers only 1941, when Kerouac was turning out huge amounts of writing, and part 3 goes up to 1943 and finishes with an extended selection from a draft of *The Sea Is My Brother*.

Paul Marion gathered these 15 stories together, as well as other "stories, excerpts from novels, poems, essays, sketches, plays and other work from 1936 to 1943,"[4] and published them to show the growth of the young writer Kerouac from his time in Lowell until his 21st year, when he began to meet people like William S. Burroughs who would be such an influence on his life. It is unfair to compare this early text to books like *On the Road* and *The Dharma Bums*; instead, it must be looked at in light of books like *Lonesome Traveler* and *Good Blonde and Others*.

Good Blonde and Others is a collection of about 30 different articles, stories, and essays that Kerouac completed for a variety of magazines, both men's magazines like *Nugget* and *Playboy* and also general-interest magazines like *Escapade*. Five of the stories involve what his public wanted—road trip stories—and the others include (largely unhelpful) writing advice, and most interestingly, a defense of America directed toward the hippie generation and a passionate defense of his novel *The Subterraneans* following its obscenity trial in Italy.

Kerouac's work that was published after his death can be read as what Kerouac always suggested he was trying to create, one large Proustian tale. To do this, one should ignore the publication dates of the works and instead focus on the date when each work is set. Readers approaching the texts in this manner would begin with *Visions of Gerard* and move on to his youth with *Dr. Sax*, then his teen years with *Maggie Cassidy*. His time at Columbia and early meetings with Ginsberg are related in *Vanity of Duluoz*, and the vital meeting with Cassady in *On the Road*, then in quick succession *Visions of Cody*, *Lonesome Traveler*, and *The Subterraneans*. These are followed by his time in Mexico City with *Tristessa*, then *The Dharma Bums* and *Desolation Angels*. His later years and slow deterioration are detailed in *Big Sur* and finally *Satori in Paris*.

In death, controversy still haunts the Kerouac name. The daughter whom he would never admit to fathering, Jan Kerouac, became a respected novelist after years as a junkie and prostitute before dying unexpectedly. Little Paul, Carolyn's son, whom Jack loved so dearly, has been homeless now off and on for more than five years. Jan and Paul Jr. both became embroiled in a controversy over Kerouac's estate. When Jack died, his estate went to his mother. When she died, a will surfaced leaving everything to Stella Sampas.

This seemed unbelievable to many. There is a letter in existence, for example, from Kerouac to Little Paul in which he says that when his mother dies, he wants everything to go to Paul, a blood relative, and states specifically that he does not want Stella or her family to get any of it. Whether or not Kerouac was in sound mind when writing the letter, just 24 hours before his death, is also still being debated. Even the Sampas family felt this was odd, because Gabrielle had never shown anything but animosity toward Stella, frequently calling her, even when the woman was nursing her, "Jack's Trash." When the witness to the will admitted that he never actually saw Gabrielle Kerouac sign it, Jan Kerouac jumped in with a lawsuit, which, at the time of this writing, had not yet been resolved. Certainly, many Kerouac scholars and friends are not happy at the way the archive has been shut off and about the fact that the letter collections and forthcoming journal collections must be approved by the Sampas family before publication.

At the time of his death, Kerouac had fallen out of critical favor in America (although his reputation in Europe was and continues to be very strong; his books remained in print in European editions even after they had long gone out of print in his native land). However, by the early to mid-1990s, Kerouac's work (as well as plenty of biographies and critical studies) was back in print, and his image was also appearing in advertisements for clothing stores like the Gap and Internet bookstores like Alibris.com.

Carl Malmgren, in his essay "*On the Road* Reconsidered," relates the story "of a conference in Boulder, Colorado, in the summer of 1982 to celebrate the twenty-fifth anniversary of the publication of Jack Kerouac's *On the Road*. In the brochure advertising the week-long multi-media 'event,' various novelists, poets and critics paid tribute to Kerouac's literary accomplishments.... William Tallman asserts that 'you've got to get past Jack to get down to writing in our time.' James Laughlin states, 'I think he was a turning point in the history of Modern American fiction.' And the poet Ted Berrigan goes so far as to say, 'I think that only with the arrival of Jack Kerouac did American Fiction become American.' "[5]

Today Kerouac fans can even go to his hometown of Lowell, Massachusetts, to take in the Jack Kerouac Commemorative—a series of eight granite blocks along Eastern Canal Park with passages from his books engraved on them—or visitors can see the rucksack, notebooks, and typewriters he took on his trips to the American West. Even with the Nicosia-Sampas lawsuit unresolved, Kerouac's previously unpublished work continues to trickle out to varying degrees of critical reception, just as during his life. His work and life continues to haunt readers and writers providing cautionary tales and inspiration for generation after generation.

NOTES

1. Ann Charters, *Kerouac* (San Francisco: Straight Arrow Books, 1973), p. 359.

2. Aram Sardyan, introduction to *Orpheus Emerged*, by Jack Kerouac (New York: I-Books, 2002), ebook.

3. Regina Weinreich, forward to *Book of Haikus*, by Jack Kerouac (New York: Penguin, 2003), p. 4.

4. Paul Marion, ed., *Atop and Underwood* (New York: Viking, 1999), p. 8.

5. Carl D. Malmgren, "*On the Road* Reconsidered: Kerouac and the Modernist Tradition." *Ball State University Forum* 30, no. 1 (Winter 1989): p. 62.

SELECTED BIBLIOGRAPHY

WORKS BY JACK KEROUAC

Atop an Underwood. New York: Viking, 1999.
Big Sur. New York: Farrar, Straus and Cudahy, 1962.
Book of Dreams. San Francisco: City Lights Books, 1961.
Desolation Angels. New York: Coward-McCann, 1965.
The Dharma Bums. New York: Viking, 1958.
Dr. Sax: Faust Part Three. New York: Grove, 1959.
Good Blonde and Others. San Francisco: Grey Fox, 1993.
Heaven and Other Poems. Bolinas, Calif.: Grey Fox, 1977.
Letters. 2 vols. New York: Viking Penguin, 1994.
Lonesome Traveler. New York: McGraw-Hill, 1960.
Maggie Cassidy. New York: Avon Books, 1959.
Mexico City Blues. New York: Grove, 1959.
Old Angel Midnight. San Francisco: Grey Fox, 1993.
On the Road. New York: Viking, 1957.
Orpheus Emerged. New York: Ibooks, 2002, ebook.
Pic. New York: Grove, 1971.
Pomes All Sizes. San Francisco: City Lights Books, 1992.
Pull My Daisy. New York: Grove, 1961.
Satori in Paris. New York: Grove, 1966.
Scattered Poems. San Francisco: City Lights Books, 1971.
The Scripture of the Golden Eternity. New York: Totem/Corinth, 1960.
Some of the Dharma. New York: Viking, 1995.
The Subterraneans. New York: Grove, 1958.
The Town and the City. New York: Harcourt, Brace, 1950.

Tristessa. New York: Avon Books, 1960.
Two Early Stories. New York: Aloe Editions, 1973.
Vanity of Duluoz: An Adventurous Education. New York: Coward-McCann, 1968.
Visions of Cody. New York: McGraw-Hill, 1972.
Visions of Gerard. New York: Farrar, Straus, 1963.

BOOKS ABOUT JACK KEROUAC

Cassady, Carolyn. *Off the Road.* New York: William Morrow, 1990.
Cassady, Carolyn, and David Sandison. *Jack Kerouac: An Illustrated Biography.* Chicago: Chicago Review, 1999.
Charters, Ann. *Kerouac.* San Francisco: Straight Arrow Books, 1973.
Charters, Ann, and Tim Hunt. *Kerouac's Crooked Road: Development of a Fiction.* Berkeley: University of California Press, 1996.
French, Warren. *Jack Kerouac.* Boston: Twayne, 1986.
Holman, C., and William Harman, eds. *A Handbook to Literature.* New York: Prentice Hall, 1996.
Holton, Robert. *On the Road: Kerouac's Ragged American Journey.* Twayne's Masterwork Studies, no. 172. Boston: Twayne, 1999.
Johnson, Joyce. *Minor Characters.* Boston: Houghton Mifflin, 1983.
McDarrah, Fred. *Kerouac and Friends: A Beat Generation Album.* New York: William Morrow, 1985.
Nicosia, Gerald. *Memory Babe: A Critical Biography of Jack Kerouac.* Berkeley: University of California Press, 1984.
Phillips, Rodney. *The Hand of the Poet.* New York: Rizzoli, 1997.
Weinreich, Regina. *The Spontaneous Poetics of Jack Kerouac: A Study of the Fiction.* Carbondale: Southern Illinois University Press, 1987.

BIOGRAPHICAL FILM

Jack Kerouac. Dir. John Antonelli. 1984.

PERIODICALS ABOUT JACK KEROUAC

Campbell, James. "Kerouac's Blues." *Antioch Review* 59 (2001): 451–58.
Eburne, Jonathan Paul. "Trafficking in the Void: Burroughs, Kerouac, and the Consumption of Otherness." *Modern Fiction Studies* 43, no. 1 (1997): 53–92.
Malmgren, Carl D. "*On the Road* Reconsidered: Kerouac and the Modernist Tradition." *Ball State University Forum* 30 (1989): 59–67. Reprinted in

Twentieth-Century Literary Criticism, vol. 117, ed. Linda Pavloski and Scott Darga (Detroit: Gale, 2002).

Mullins, Patrick. "Hollywood and the Beats." *Journal of Popular Film and Television* (Spring 2001): 32–42.

Wilson, Steve. " 'Buddha Writing': The Author and the Search for Authenticity in Jack Kerouac's *On the Road* and *The Subterraneans*." *Midwest Quarterly* 40 (1999): 302–15.

INTERNET SOURCES

Asher, Levi. "Jack Kerouac." http://www.charm.net/~brooklyn/People/Jack Kerouac.html.

Brinkley, Douglas. "In the Kerouac Archive." http://www.theatlantic.com/issues/98nov/kerouac.htm.

Gallaher, Tim. "Sounds of Jack Kerouac Reading (and Singing) His Prose." http://www-hsc.usc.edu/~gallaher/k_speaks/kerouacspeaks.html.

Gyenis, Attila. "Dharma Beat." http://members.aol.com/kerouaczin/dharmabeat.html.

"Jack Kerouac's Roads." Department of English and American Studies, Vienna University. http://www.univie.ac.at/Anglistik/easyrider/data/picks_on_kerouac.htm.

"Official Web Site of Jack Kerouac." http://www.cmgww.com/historic/kerouac/.

Rumsey, Ken. "The Beat Page—Jack Kerouac." http://www.rooknet.com/beatpage/writers/kerouac.html.

Trondson-Clinger, Eric. "Kerouac Character Key." http://www.charm.net/~brooklyn/Lists/KerouacNames.html.

INDEX

About the Author

MICHAEL J. DITTMAN teaches English at Clarion University of Penn-sylvania. He has published poetry and has contributed critical articles for *Contemporary American Women Poets* (Greenwood, 2001) and *American Literature Archive*.